Type 2 Diabetes Cookbook for Beginners

1800 Days of Simple, Tasty, and Nutrient-Rich Recipes - Comes with a Detailed 30-Day Meal Plan

By Ava Belle

Table of Contents

Introduction

Living with Type 2 Diabetes is a journey filled with challenges and opportunities. It's a path that demands a profound understanding of one's body, a radical transformation in lifestyle, and an unwavering commitment to health and wellbeing. As those diagnosed with this condition know, it's not just about numbers, charts, and medical jargon; it's about life, food, family, and the art of enjoying each day to its fullest.

As the prevalence of Type 2 Diabetes continues to grow, so does the need for comprehensive and compassionate guidance. Whether you're newly diagnosed or seeking to deepen your understanding of managing this condition, the world of diabetes-friendly living can often feel overwhelming. Questions about what to eat, how to cook, when to exercise, and even how to enjoy your favorite foods without harm can create confusion and anxiety.

This is where this comprehensive guide, woven with the essence of science, culinary arts, and compassionate understanding, comes into play. Chapter 1 sets the stage for an empowering journey towards a healthier, happier, and more flavorful life. Here's what you can expect:

1. **Understanding Type 2 Diabetes: The Basics** - A deep dive into what Type 2 Diabetes is, how it affects the body, and what it means for daily living. This section is not about medicalizing the condition; it's about humanizing it, making it accessible, and relating it to everyday life.

2. **The Importance of Diet in Managing Type 2 Diabetes** - Food is not just fuel; it's a friend, a healer, and a joy-bringer. This section explores how diet plays a crucial role in managing Type 2 Diabetes and how it can be embraced with creativity and enjoyment.

3. **How This Cookbook Can Help: A Brief Overview** - This cookbook is more than a collection of recipes; it's a guide, a companion, and an inspirer. Here, you'll see how this cookbook will walk with you, teach you, and celebrate with you as you embrace a diabetes-friendly lifestyle.

With the synthesis of scientific insights, practical tips, culinary creativity, and compassionate understanding, Chapter 1 invites you to step into a world where Type 2 Diabetes is not a limit but a launchpad. It's a world where food is celebrated, life is embraced, and every day offers an opportunity to grow, learn, and love.

Understanding Type 2 Diabetes: The Basics

Type 2 Diabetes is a multifaceted condition that affects millions worldwide. Understanding it requires delving into the intricacies of our body's systems, behaviors, and genetics. Let's explore these dimensions:

Type 2 Diabetes is marked by insulin resistance. To comprehend this, imagine your cells are locked rooms, and insulin is the key to open them. In insulin resistance, these keys are less effective, causing the sugar to remain in the blood rather than fueling cells.

The reasons behind this resistance are complex:

Cell Receptor Changes: The 'locks' on cells that insulin fits into can become altered, making it more challenging for insulin to open the door.

Inflammatory Factors: Chronic inflammation in the body may interfere with insulin's ability to function, contributing to resistance.

Fatty Acid Build-Up: Excessive fatty acids in the blood might impede insulin's effectiveness.

While genetic factors play a role, lifestyle choices often have a significant impact:

Diet: Diets high in refined carbohydrates and unhealthy fats might accelerate insulin resistance.

Physical Activity: Regular exercise makes the body more receptive to insulin. Lack of it can contribute to Type 2 Diabetes.

One of the most insidious aspects of Type 2 Diabetes is that it often progresses quietly. People may live with the condition for years without knowing it. This silent progression can lead to complications like heart disease, kidney failure, and nerve damage.

Being diagnosed with Type 2 Diabetes can be overwhelming. It demands a radical reassessment of daily habits and routines:

Dietary Changes: Understanding carbohydrates, sugars, and fats becomes essential. The joy of eating must be balanced with the practicality of managing blood sugar levels.

Lifestyle Shifts: Regular exercise, monitoring blood sugar, taking medications, and attending medical appointments become integral parts of life.

Type 2 Diabetes doesn't exist in a vacuum; it intersects with societal and economic factors:

Healthcare Access: Access to diagnosis, treatment, and ongoing care can be barriers for many.

Community Support: Local community support and understanding can significantly impact how an individual copes with the disease.

Understanding Type 2 Diabetes is more than understanding a medical condition; it's about comprehending a way of life that intertwines with the very fabric of our being. It involves recognizing the symbiotic relationship between our bodies, the food we consume, our daily habits, our mental state, and our place within our community.
This book aims to be more than a cookbook; it seeks to be a companion on this journey, offering not only delicious recipes but also insights, encouragement, and empowerment. By embracing this understanding, we can move beyond viewing Type 2 Diabetes as a limitation and see it as an opportunity to rediscover ourselves, our health, and the joy of nourishing our bodies.

In the subsequent chapters, we'll explore practical aspects like setting up your kitchen, understanding food labels, and discovering delightful recipes that align with the needs of managing Type 2 Diabetes. But most importantly, this book serves as an affirmation that you have the power to thrive, enjoy, and lead a fulfilling life, all while managing Type 2 Diabetes effectively.

While lifestyle plays a critical role, genetics cannot be ignored. Type 2 Diabetes often runs in families, with certain genetic markers being associated with a higher risk:
Family History: Those with a family history of diabetes are more likely to develop the condition.
Ethnic Background: Some ethnic groups have a higher propensity for Type 2 Diabetes, including African, Hispanic, Asian, and Native American populations.
Understanding one's genetic risk factors can lead to early intervention and better management of the condition.

Metabolic Syndrome refers to a cluster of conditions that increase the risk of heart disease, stroke, and Type 2 Diabetes. These conditions include high blood pressure, high blood sugar, excess body fat around the waist, and abnormal cholesterol levels. Understanding how these factors interact and contribute to insulin resistance helps create a more comprehensive approach to prevention and management.

Knowing that Type 2 Diabetes can often be prevented or delayed through early intervention, focusing on preventative measures is vital:

Weight Management: Keeping weight within a healthy range can prevent or delay the onset.
Healthy Eating Habits: Integrating more whole foods, fiber, and healthy fats can contribute to prevention.
Regular Physical Activity: Exercise not only aids in weight control but improves

insulin sensitivity.

Monitoring and Managing Blood Sugar Levels

Living with Type 2 Diabetes means regularly monitoring blood sugar levels:

Understanding Glucose Monitoring: The tools, techniques, and timing for effective monitoring.

Identifying Patterns and Trends: Keeping a log and recognizing how different foods and activities affect blood sugar.

Reacting to Highs and Lows: Understanding how to respond to fluctuations in blood sugar, including dealing with hypoglycemia or hyperglycemia.

For many, managing Type 2 Diabetes involves medication:

Oral Medications: There are different classes of oral diabetes medications, each working differently to control blood sugar.

Insulin Therapy: Some may require insulin injections or pumps.

Alternative Treatments: Complementary therapies like herbal supplements or acupuncture may be considered, but they must be discussed with healthcare providers.

The Importance of Diet in Managing Type 2 Diabetes

The plate in front of you may not seem like a medical tool, but if you have Type 2 Diabetes, food becomes an essential part of your treatment plan. The choices you make in the kitchen, at the grocery store, and even in restaurants have a profound impact on your well-being, far beyond satisfying hunger.

Managing Type 2 Diabetes through diet isn't just about avoiding sugar or counting carbohydrates. It's about nourishing your body in a way that minimizes blood sugar spikes, promotes healthy weight, and supports overall health. Let's break down why diet is so fundamental in controlling this condition:

The Connection between Food and Blood Sugar

The relationship between food and blood sugar is a complex dance, especially for those with Type 2 Diabetes. This connection requires more than merely a passing glance; it demands a deep understanding of how different foods affect the body's sugar levels. Here's a comprehensive look at this vital link:

When we eat, the digestive system breaks down food into various nutrients, including glucose, a simple sugar that acts as the body's main energy source. In healthy individuals, the hormone insulin helps cells absorb glucose, but for those with Type 2 Diabetes, insulin resistance can disrupt this process.

The Impact of Different Nutrients

Carbohydrates: These are the primary source of glucose, and not all are created equal. Simple carbohydrates like sugars can cause rapid spikes in blood sugar, while complex carbohydrates like whole grains release glucose more slowly, providing steadier energy.

Proteins and Fats: Though primarily not sources of glucose, they can affect how the body processes carbohydrates. Including protein and fat with a carbohydrate-rich meal can slow down the absorption of glucose, leading to a more gentle rise in blood sugar.

Understanding the glycemic index (GI) and glycemic load (GL) can help manage blood sugar levels. The GI measures how quickly a particular food raises blood sugar, while the GL considers both the GI and the amount of carbohydrate in the food. Lower GI and GL foods are generally more favorable for maintaining stable blood sugar levels. Monitoring and Responding

Careful monitoring of blood sugar levels is essential for understanding how different foods and meals affect an individual. Continuous learning, adjusting, and being mindful of the body's responses enable a tailored approach to managing Type 2 Diabetes.

Carbohydrates: The Energy Source

Complex Over Simple: Opting for complex carbohydrates like whole grains, legumes, and vegetables, allows for a slower release of glucose.

Portion Control: Understanding portion sizes for carbohydrates helps to avoid unintended blood sugar spikes.

Proteins: Building and Satisfying

Lean Choices: Choosing lean proteins like poultry, fish, and plant-based options helps manage weight and satisfies hunger without excess saturated fat.

Complementary Role: Protein aids in the slower absorption of glucose, providing a stabilizing effect on blood sugar levels.

Fats: The Heart of the Matter

Healthy Selections: Fats like avocados, nuts, and olive oil provide essential fatty acids and support heart health, a vital consideration for those with Type 2 Diabetes.

Avoiding Trans Fats: Trans fats can increase insulin resistance and should be avoided.

Vitamins and Minerals: Supporting Players
Micronutrients Matter: Ensuring adequate intake of vitamins and minerals like magnesium and Vitamin D supports overall health, including insulin sensitivity.
Colorful Choices: A colorful plate with various fruits and vegetables provides a spectrum of vitamins, minerals, and fiber, enhancing overall diet quality.

Balancing nutrients is not a one-size-fits-all approach. It must align with an individual's lifestyle, preferences, and health needs. Working with healthcare providers, using tools like food diaries, and being open to experimentation can create a nutrient symphony that supports both health and pleasure in eating.
In the complex world of Type 2 Diabetes management, understanding these principles helps transform the daily act of eating from a source of anxiety into a joyful and nourishing experience. By deepening our connection with food and blood sugar and mastering the art of nutrient balance, we empower ourselves to thrive with diabetes.

With Type 2 Diabetes, quantity is as important as quality. Understanding portion sizes helps prevent overeating and manages blood sugar spikes. But portion control is not about deprivation; it's about enjoying a variety of foods in moderation.
The Power of Meal Timing
Eating at consistent intervals can stabilize blood sugar levels. Regular meals and snacks can prevent dramatic highs and lows that can affect mood, energy levels, and overall health.

For many with Type 2 Diabetes, weight management is a significant aspect of controlling the condition. Excess weight, particularly around the waist, can lead to increased insulin resistance. A tailored diet can:

- **Encourage Weight Loss if Needed**: A balanced diet that emphasizes nutrient-dense, lower-calorie foods can support healthy weight loss.
- **Maintain a Healthy Weight**: Once a healthy weight is reached, continued mindful eating can sustain it.

Managing Type 2 Diabetes through diet is not about restriction; it's about making choices that nourish the body. It's about:

- **Discovering New Tastes**: Experimenting with fresh ingredients and new recipes.
- **Celebrating Meals**: Taking joy in preparation and sharing meals with loved ones.
- **Listening to Your Body**: Recognizing hunger and fullness cues and responding appropriately.

A registered dietitian or certified diabetes care and education specialist can offer personalized recommendations based on individual needs, preferences, and medical history.

- **Individualized Meal Planning**: Working together to create a plan that suits your lifestyle and preferences.

- **Education and Support**: Understanding the why and how of dietary choices, plus ongoing support to adapt and grow.

Food is more than fuel; it's a part of culture, celebration, and comfort. Integrating diabetes-friendly eating into your life requires attention to these aspects:

- **Honoring Traditions**: Adapting favorite family recipes to be more diabetes-friendly.

- **Navigating Social Gatherings**: Making informed choices without feeling isolated or deprived.

The importance of diet in managing Type 2 Diabetes cannot be overstated. It's a science and an art, a challenge and a joy. Through these pages, you'll learn not only the principles of diabetes-friendly eating but how to apply them in delicious and satisfying ways.

In this cookbook, you'll find recipes, techniques, and insights that cater to your unique journey with Type 2 Diabetes. From a steamy bowl of oatmeal that warms your morning to a succulent piece of grilled fish that stars in your dinner, every dish is a step towards better health.

As we delve into the subsequent chapters, you'll see that managing Type 2 Diabetes with diet is not about sacrificing flavor or joy. It's about embracing food as a partner in health, exploring new tastes, and nourishing yourself with every delicious bite.

Your fork, indeed, is one of the most powerful tools you have in managing your diabetes, and together we'll learn how to wield it with wisdom, creativity, and delight.

How This Cookbook Can Help: A Brief Overview

Managing Type 2 Diabetes is a complex task that demands more than mere adherence to medication. It calls for a life-altering transformation, a radical shift in dietary habits, and a profound understanding of how different foods play with one's blood sugar levels. And yet, for many, this path is fraught with uncertainties, confusion, and the fear of letting go of beloved culinary traditions. This is where this cookbook steps in as a guide, a friend, and a culinary artist, easing the transition into a world where food is both a delight and a healer. Here's how this cookbook promises to assist you on this journey.

From Confusion to Clarity: Demystifying Diabetes Cooking

Diabetes-friendly cooking often comes wrapped in myths and misconceptions. Is it all about cutting out sugars? Is it a bland, unappetizing journey that robs food of its joy? This cookbook dispels these myths by embracing science and culinary creativity, making the path clear and the journey delightful.

Structuring Your Path: The 30-Day Meal Plan

Embarking on a new dietary lifestyle can be overwhelming. What to eat? When to eat? How much to eat? The questions are endless. The 30-Day Meal Plan within this cookbook is designed as a structured yet flexible guide, easing you into the world of diabetes-friendly eating. By offering day-by-day suggestions, it simplifies the process, allowing you to focus on enjoying your meals rather than stressing over them.

Your Kitchen, Your Laboratory: Essential Techniques and Ingredients

Understanding cooking techniques and essential pantry staples can transform your kitchen from a mere food-preparation space into a laboratory of flavor, health, and creativity. This cookbook introduces you to cooking techniques ranging from steaming to sautéing, and highlights the vital ingredients that will become the cornerstone of your diabetes-friendly kitchen.

Recipes to Delight: Breakfast to Dessert

The rich collection of recipes within this cookbook is not merely a list of dishes; it's a celebration of taste, tradition, and innovation. Whether you crave a hearty breakfast, a sumptuous lunch, or a comforting dinner, this cookbook has something to offer. From poultry and fish to vegetarian and low-carb options, the choices are versatile and adaptable to your preferences.

Special Sections for Special Needs

Life is not one-size-fits-all, and neither is this cookbook. With sections devoted to quick and easy recipes for busy days, plant-based options for vegetarians, and high-fiber recipes for digestive health, it acknowledges and respects the diversity of its readers, offering something for every unique need and desire.

Beyond Food: A Holistic Approach
The cookbook doesn't stop at food. It extends its hand into the broader aspects of diabetes management, such as physical activity and stress management. Recognizing that food is but one part of a multifaceted lifestyle, it offers insights into exercise tips, mindfulness techniques, and regular health check-ups, creating a comprehensive guide to a balanced lifestyle.

Resources, Appendices, and Support
With glossaries, shopping lists, substitution charts, and recommended brands, this cookbook ensures that you are never alone or unsupported in this journey. It functions not just as a collection of recipes but as a constant companion that you can refer to, lean on, and grow with.

Embracing Joy, Confidence, and Control
Perhaps the most beautiful offering of this cookbook is the joy, confidence, and control it instills. With every page turned, every dish tried, and every success tasted, it empowers you to reclaim control over your health, infuse joy into your meals, and build confidence in your ability to manage diabetes.

As we conclude Chapter 1, we hope that you feel a sense of empowerment, clarity, and excitement. Understanding Type 2 Diabetes is not just about recognizing a medical condition; it's about embracing a lifestyle that can be rich, fulfilling, and joyous. It's about seeing food not as an enemy but as an ally, a creator of flavors, a bringer of family together, and a sustainer of life.

Through the exploration of the basics of Type 2 Diabetes, the profound importance of diet, and the multifaceted offerings of this cookbook, Chapter 1 has laid the foundation for a journey that is both practical and poetic. It's a journey that acknowledges the challenges but focuses on the opportunities, that respects the science but celebrates the art, that understands the fear but emphasizes the joy.

The path ahead is rich with recipes, techniques, insights, and support, all designed to make your journey with Type 2 Diabetes not just manageable but enjoyable. Whether you are at the beginning of this path or further along, this cookbook and guide offer a hand, a heart, and a promise. A promise to walk with you, to cook with you, to laugh and learn with you.

May you find in these pages not just information but inspiration, not just **Directions** but connections, not just food but fulfillment. Welcome to a world where Type 2 Diabetes is not a full stop but a comma, a pause that invites reflection, adaptation, and a beautiful continuation. Here's to a life well-lived, well-loved, and well-fed. Here's to you.

Chapter 2: Getting Started

Welcome to the crucial stage of your journey with type 2 diabetes - getting started with the right approach to food, cooking, and overall wellness. This chapter is your gateway to understanding not just the mechanics of cooking, but also the art and philosophy behind it. It's about creating an environment and approach to food that respects your body's needs and your taste buds' desires.

For many with type 2 diabetes, the kitchen may seem like a battleground. There's a constant struggle between what you crave and what you need, what tastes good and what's good for you. But it doesn't have to be this way. With the right tools, techniques, and mindset, the kitchen can become a sanctuary, a place of healing and enjoyment.

We start this chapter with the essentials. Understanding the tools and pantry staples lays the groundwork for everything that follows. It's about building your culinary toolkit with equipment that makes cooking easier, and stocking your pantry with ingredients that are both wholesome and flavorful. A well-organized kitchen fosters creativity and reduces stress, turning cooking from a chore into a pleasure.

Next, we delve into cooking techniques, from the gentle art of steaming to the quick and vibrant method of sautéing. These techniques are more than mere instructions; they're gateways to understanding food, its texture, taste, and nutritional value. Cooking methods can make or break a dish, and they can also make or break your diet. Hence, knowing the right techniques is pivotal to managing your diabetes without sacrificing the joy of eating.

Lastly, we demystify food labels, breaking down what they mean and how to use them to your advantage. This is about empowering you to make informed choices, not just about sugar and carbs but about understanding the overall nutritional landscape. When you know what goes into your food, you can make decisions that align with your goals, tastes, and values.

Together, these elements form the backbone of your culinary adventure. They are building blocks that turn the act of cooking from mere sustenance into a form of self-care, a way to nourish not just your body, but your soul.

The journey through this chapter is akin to setting up a garden. You'll cultivate the soil (your kitchen), plant the seeds (the right tools and ingredients), nurture the growth (learning techniques), and finally, enjoy the fruits of your labor (delicious, healthful meals).

Setting Up Your Kitchen: Essential Tools and Pantry Staples

The Heart of Your Home

The kitchen, often referred to as the heart of the home, is a place where memories are made, laughter echoes, and nourishment thrives. As you embark on your journey towards a diabetes-friendly lifestyle, your kitchen must transform into a sanctuary that aids you in this significant life change. By carefully selecting the tools and ingredients that occupy this space, you create an environment that supports your health and wellness goals.

Tools for Success

A well-equipped kitchen is the first step towards successful meal planning and preparation. It doesn't mean that your kitchen needs to resemble a professional chef's workstation, but having essential tools readily available makes the process more enjoyable and less daunting.

Knives

Chef's Knife: An all-purpose knife used for chopping, dicing, and mincing. It's a versatile tool for cutting vegetables, meats, and herbs.

Paring Knife: Smaller in size, it's perfect for peeling and cutting small fruits and vegetables.

Bread Knife: Serrated to cut through bread without crushing it, useful for whole-grain bread that forms part of a diabetes-friendly diet.

Cutting Boards

Wooden Cutting Board: Suitable for cutting fruits and vegetables; it's sturdy and won't dull knives quickly.

Plastic Cutting Board: Often used for cutting meats, as it's easy to sanitize.

Measuring Tools

Measuring Cups and Spoons: Vital for portion control and accurate ingredient measurements, both of which are essential for managing blood sugar levels.

Kitchen Scale: Allows for precise weighing of ingredients, aiding in consistent portion sizes.

Cooking Utensils

Non-Stick Skillet: Useful for cooking with less oil, aligning with a heart-healthy diet.

Spatulas and Tongs: For flipping and turning foods, providing control while cooking.

Whisks and Mixing Spoons: Essential for mixing ingredients and ensuring proper blending of flavors.

Small Appliances
Blender: For smoothies and pureeing soups, allowing for more homemade and nutrient-dense options.
Slow Cooker: Encourages cooking in bulk with controlled, low-fat methods.
Food Processor: Helpful in quickly chopping vegetables or blending ingredients, saving time and effort.

Bakeware
Baking Sheets: Useful for roasting vegetables or baking proteins, a method that requires less added fat.
Muffin Tins: Great for portion-controlled meals and snacks.

Specialized Tools
Steamer Basket: Enables healthy cooking through steaming, preserving nutrients in vegetables.
Grater: Allows for grating fresh ingredients like ginger or zucchini, adding flavor without additional sugars or salts.
Oil Spritzer: Controls the amount of oil used in cooking, contributing to a heart-healthy approach.
Insulated Food Thermos: Handy for packing healthy, homemade lunches, encouraging better meal choices on the go.
Instant-Read Thermometer: Ensures meats are cooked to the proper temperature, promoting food safety.

Storage Solutions
Airtight Containers: Vital for storing prepped meals and leftovers, facilitating meal planning and portion control.
By investing in these kitchen tools, you set the stage for easier, more efficient cooking tailored to the needs of a diabetes-friendly diet. Each tool plays a role in facilitating healthy cooking practices, encouraging portion control, and making the cooking process more enjoyable and manageable.

Pantry Essentials
A pantry stocked with essential ingredients is like a painter's palette filled with colors; it provides the base for creating culinary masterpieces that not only delight your taste buds but also align with your diabetes management goals.

Whole Grains
Whole grains are an excellent source of fiber, which helps regulate blood sugar levels.

By replacing refined grains with whole grains, you support a slower release of glucose into the bloodstream.

Brown Rice: Unlike white rice, brown rice retains its outer layer, providing more fiber and nutrients.

Quinoa: Rich in protein, quinoa is a gluten-free grain that cooks quickly and offers a nutty flavor.

Whole Wheat Pasta: A great alternative to regular pasta, it delivers more fiber and keeps you full for longer.

Barley: Barley is another whole grain rich in soluble fiber, known for its ability to help control blood sugar levels.

Healthy Oils

Cooking with healthy oils that contain unsaturated fats supports heart health, a significant consideration for those with Type 2 diabetes.

Olive Oil: Known for its heart-healthy properties, olive oil is a staple in Mediterranean cooking.

Avocado Oil: With a higher smoke point, avocado oil is excellent for cooking at higher temperatures, and it offers monounsaturated fats.

Herbs and Spices

Spices and herbs can elevate a dish without adding salt or sugar, and some even have health-promoting properties.

Cinnamon: This sweet spice may help improve insulin sensitivity.

Turmeric: Known for its anti-inflammatory properties, turmeric adds a vibrant color to dishes.

Garlic: Garlic is flavorful and might have benefits for heart health.

Lean Proteins

Protein is a vital part of a balanced diet and helps maintain muscle mass and repair tissues.

Canned Chicken or Turkey: These provide quick and easy protein options for salads, soups, or sandwiches.

Fish: Canned or frozen fish like salmon and tuna are rich in omega-3 fatty acids, important for heart health.

Beans: Canned or dried beans provide plant-based protein, fiber, and nutrients without added fats.

Vegetables and Fruits
Having a variety of vegetables and fruits ensures you have access to essential vitamins, minerals, and dietary fiber.

Frozen Vegetables: They retain most of their nutrients and are ready to cook.

Canned Fruits: Choose those packed in water or natural juices to avoid added sugars.

Nuts and Seeds
These nutrient-dense options provide healthy fats and are satisfying snacks or additions to meals.

Almonds: High in monounsaturated fats, almonds can be a satisfying snack.

Chia Seeds: These tiny seeds are packed with fiber and omega-3 fatty acids.

Sugar Substitutes
Sugar substitutes can help satisfy sweet cravings without affecting blood sugar levels.

Stevia: A natural, zero-calorie sweetener derived from the leaves of the Stevia plant.

Monk Fruit: Another natural sweetener, monk fruit extract is sweeter than sugar but without the calories.

Erythritol: A sugar alcohol that tastes similar to sugar but has minimal impact on blood sugar levels.

The Philosophy of Mindfulness
Cultivating a mindful kitchen is about embracing a holistic approach to cooking and the space in which it happens. It's not just about having the right tools and ingredients, but creating an environment that nourishes the mind, body, and soul. For someone managing diabetes, this can be an empowering way to take control of their diet and well-being.

Inspiring Creativity
Personalized Touches: Adding elements that reflect your personality and interests can make the kitchen a place of inspiration. Artwork, decorative utensils, or even your favorite colors can spark creativity.

Open Space for Experimentation: Design the kitchen layout so that it's comfortable to move and experiment with recipes. A spacious countertop can provide room to explore new dishes that align with diabetes-friendly eating.

Evoking Joy
Natural Light: If possible, letting in natural sunlight can lift the mood and energize the space. Sunshine can make the kitchen feel warm and inviting.

Plants and Fresh Herbs: Incorporating greenery or a small herb garden in the kitchen can add life and freshness. It also encourages the use of fresh herbs, enhancing flavors without added salt or sugar.

Facilitating Wellness
Strategic Organization: Placing tools and ingredients in easily accessible locations encourages cooking at home. If whole grains, fresh vegetables, and lean proteins are within reach, it's easier to cook meals that support blood sugar management.

Hygiene and Cleanliness: A clean kitchen promotes a healthy cooking environment. Regular cleaning practices ensure that food preparation is hygienic, which is especially important when managing a specific diet.

Pleasure over Chore
Enjoyable Routine: Designing a cooking routine that you enjoy can turn meal preparation from a chore into a satisfying part of your day. Cooking can become a time to unwind and reconnect with food and your nutritional needs.

Community and Connection: If space allows, creating a welcoming environment for family and friends can turn cooking and eating into a communal, joyful experience. Sharing meals can reinforce positive eating habits and provide support in managing diabetes.

Mindful Eating
Connection with Food: Understanding and respecting the ingredients and the process of cooking fosters a deeper connection to what you eat. Mindful eating practices encourage slower, more thoughtful eating, supporting digestion and better blood sugar control.

Essential Cooking Techniques: From Steaming to Sautéing

Introduction to Cooking Techniques
Cooking is an art that brings joy, creativity, and nourishment. For individuals managing type 2 diabetes, knowing the right cooking techniques can be a powerful ally in maintaining a healthy and balanced diet. This chapter will guide you through essential cooking methods that can turn simple ingredients into delightful meals that not only taste good but support your well-being.

The Art of Steaming
Steaming is a gentle way to cook food, preserving the nutrients and colors of vegetables and proteins. For a person with diabetes, this method helps retain the vitamins in vegetables that are critical to health.

Steaming: Preserving Nutrients and Freshness
Steaming is a gentle cooking technique that preserves the integrity of the ingredients. It's a method that envelops food in a cloud of steam, cooking it uniformly without direct contact with water. This is a perfect technique for people with diabetes, as it keeps the essential nutrients intact.

Steaming involves cooking food by surrounding it with hot steam. This gentle heat cooks the food without removing vitamins and minerals, unlike boiling. Vegetables retain their color, texture, and taste, while proteins like chicken or fish become tender without drying out.

From a traditional bamboo steamer to a modern electric version, several tools can facilitate steaming. Even without specialized equipment, a colander over a pot of simmering water, covered with a lid, can create an effective steaming environment.

Though steaming might seem bland, you can infuse wonderful flavors by adding herbs or citrus to the steaming water. For example, adding a slice of lemon and a sprig of dill to the water while steaming fish can create a delicate and aromatic dish.

Simmering: Blending Flavors Gently
Simmering is about patience and gentle handling of food. Cooking food in liquid at temperatures just below boiling allows flavors to develop slowly and meld together beautifully. This technique is used for soups, stews, and braising meats.

Simmering involves maintaining a temperature where the liquid shows tiny bubbles, but not a full boil. This slow, gentle heat allows the ingredients to cook uniformly, and the flavors to permeate through the dish.

Monitoring and maintaining the right temperature is crucial in simmering. Too high, and you risk boiling and overcooking the food. Too low, and the food might not cook through. Using a thermometer and timing the simmer can lead to perfection. Simmering is an opportunity to build layers of flavor. Starting with a base of sautéed onions, garlic, or other aromatics, and adding herbs and spices, can create a rich, flavorful foundation for your dish.

Grilling: The Flavor of Fire
Grilling imparts a unique smoky flavor to food and creates a delightful charred texture. It's a method that's loved for its ability to cook food with minimal fat and maximum flavor.

Grilling cooks food over an open flame or heated grill grates. The intense heat quickly sears the food, locking in juices, and creating beautiful grill marks.

Marinades can enhance flavor and tenderness. For diabetes-friendly options, consider marinades made of vinegar, herbs, and spices instead of sugary sauces. Marinades not only add taste but can also help in reducing the formation of harmful compounds on grilled meats.

Grilling requires attention to cooking times and temperatures, particularly for meats. Using a meat thermometer ensures that meat reaches a safe internal temperature without overcooking.

Sautéing: Fast and Flavorful
Sautéing is about cooking quickly and efficiently. This technique is perfect for tender vegetables and lean proteins, cooking them rapidly in a small amount of healthy fat.

Sautéing involves cooking food quickly in a hot pan. The key is to keep the food moving to prevent sticking and to ensure even cooking. A wide, shallow pan, ideally non-stick, works best.

The choice of oil matters in sautéing. Oils like olive and avocado, rich in healthy fats, can enhance the taste without harming health. Combined with herbs and spices, sautéing can create dishes that are both flavorful and healthful.

The art of sautéing lies in understanding the balance between heat, fat, and movement. Too hot, and the food may burn. Too little movement, and it may stick. Mastery of this method comes with practice and attentiveness.

Decoding Food Labels: Understanding Nutritional Information and Ingredients

Navigating the nutritional information panel can feel like deciphering a foreign language, but with a little guidance, it becomes a valuable tool in controlling your blood sugar levels.

Start by examining the calories and serving sizes. The number of calories is based on a standard serving size, so compare this to what you would usually eat. Sometimes what's considered a single serving on a package might be much less than what you'd typically consume. For someone with type 2 diabetes, the total carbohydrate content, including sugars and fiber, is vital. Look for foods that have lower sugar content and higher fiber content, as fiber can help slow down the absorption of sugar and thus help control blood glucose levels. Though the focus is often on sugar and carbs, don't overlook the fat, protein, and sodium content. Healthy fats are essential but should be consumed in moderation. Protein content is also significant, especially if you're trying to build or maintain muscle mass. Sodium, on the other hand, should be limited, particularly if you have high blood pressure. The ingredients list, usually found next to or below the nutrition facts panel, is equally vital. It's not just about the nutrients but also what's used to deliver those nutrients.

Ingredients are listed by quantity, from most to least. If sugar or unhealthy fats are among the first few ingredients, that's a red flag. Sometimes, sugar and unhealthy fats lurk behind scientific names. Words like "sucrose," "glucose," "fructose," and "hydrogenated oils" can be confusing but are essential to recognize. Being able to identify these words can help you make better choices for your diabetes management. Whole foods, such as whole grains, are healthier options. So when you see terms like "whole grain" or "whole wheat" at the beginning of an ingredients list, it generally indicates a nutritious choice.

Understanding food labels isn't just about numbers and scientific terms; it's about translating this information into real-world choices. With practice, you'll become fluent in the language of food labels, making grocery shopping a more empowering experience.

By making sense of food labels, you can make better decisions about what to eat and how to prepare meals that suit your nutritional needs and taste preferences. In the context of type 2 diabetes, this knowledge can be a significant factor in maintaining control over the condition.

Decoding food labels is more than a practical skill; it's a fundamental part of managing your health and enjoying food that nourishes both your body and soul. Remember, the more you understand about what's in the food you eat, the more control you have over your health.

With this newfound knowledge, you can enter the grocery store with confidence, knowing that you have the tools to make informed, healthy decisions. No longer will food labels be a cryptic code but rather a clear guide to nourishing your body in the best way possible. Your ability to understand food labels is not only a step towards better health but also a stride towards a more fulfilling and enjoyable culinary experience.

As we conclude this chapter, you've not only gathered the essential tools and ingredients but also learned to wield them with grace and understanding. The act of cooking, once daunting or tedious, has transformed into an enriching experience, filled with discovery and joy.

But more importantly, this chapter has laid a solid foundation for embracing a lifestyle that balances the demands of diabetes management with the pleasures of culinary exploration. You've learned to see beyond the numbers on food labels, understanding the story they tell about nutrition and health. You've mastered techniques that transform humble ingredients into nourishing, delicious meals.

The lessons here go beyond the stove and the plate. They reflect a mindful approach to eating, one that connects you with your food, your body, and your well-being. This isn't just about controlling blood sugar levels; it's about enhancing your quality of life. Consider your kitchen as a canvas, and these techniques, tools, and insights as colors in your palette. Each meal is a masterpiece, shaped by your choices, your efforts, and your creativity. And like any art form, cooking offers endless opportunities to learn, grow, and find satisfaction.

The path ahead is filled with delicious opportunities, from creating a 30-day meal plan that introduces variety and balance, to exploring recipes that tantalize your palate without compromising your health. This chapter is just the beginning, a solid footing on a journey that promises to be as fulfilling as it is flavorful.

And remember, this isn't just about eating right for diabetes; it's about eating right for you. It's about understanding your unique tastes and nutritional needs and crafting a culinary experience that nourishes you in every sense.

So, take these tools and techniques, and make them your own. Experiment, explore, and enjoy the process. Let your kitchen be a place of creativity, wellness, and warmth. May your meals be filled with love, your plate with color, and your life with health.

Chapter 3: The 30-Day meal Plan

Welcome to Chapter 3. The 30-Day Meal Plan. Embarking on a journey towards a diabetes-friendly lifestyle is a momentous decision, and we're here to guide you every step of the way. This chapter is divided into sections that provide a comprehensive understanding of the path to achieving control over your type 2 diabetes through mindful eating, variety, portion control, and sustainable habits. Diabetes-friendly eating doesn't mean deprivation or boredom. In fact, it can be a delicious adventure where you explore new flavors and cooking techniques while focusing on your health. We'll help you see that a variety of ingredients and a balanced diet are not only essential for your well-being but also add excitement to your plate.

We'll dive into the heart of portion control, a skill that is crucial yet often misunderstood. By mastering portions, you gain more than just control over your blood sugar levels; you also cultivate an awareness of your body's needs and satisfaction signals.

We understand that change takes time, effort, and a whole lot of confidence. So, we'll also discuss building confidence and creating sustainability in your eating habits. The importance of a supportive environment and focusing on overall health and well-being will be our guides to success.

You'll find helpful tips, day-by-day meal suggestions, and a glossary to make this journey accessible and enjoyable. Let's embark on this 30-day adventure together, embracing the joy of food and the power of conscious eating.

Week 1: Introduction to Diabetes-Friendly Eating

Welcome to the first week of your 30-Day Meal Plan. This week is about laying down the foundation and understanding what it means to eat in a way that's friendly to those with type 2 diabetes. But before we jump into a new culinary adventure, let's take a moment to demystify what diabetes-friendly eating really means.

Finding Your Footing in the World of Diabetes-Friendly Eating

It's not just about eliminating sugar; it's about balance, nutrition, and listening to your body. Having type 2 diabetes doesn't mean you are restricted to bland, tasteless food. In fact, with the right choices and a little creativity, you can enjoy a wide variety of delicious meals without compromising your health.

Understanding Carbohydrates

Carbohydrates often become the focal point of a diabetes-friendly diet. The key is understanding how different types of carbohydrates affect your blood sugar levels. Whole grains, vegetables, fruits, and legumes are sources of complex carbohydrates that provide energy without causing sudden spikes in blood sugar. These foods are rich in fiber, which helps in slower digestion and a steadier release of energy.

Proteins and Fats: Your New Allies

Proteins and healthy fats are essential components of a balanced diet. They help you feel full and provide a steady energy release, reducing the likelihood of overeating or cravings for unhealthy foods. Options like lean meats, fish, nuts, and avocados are excellent choices to incorporate into your meals.

Planning Your First Week: A New Adventure

Now that we've laid down the basic principles, planning your first week of meals becomes an exciting adventure rather than a daunting task. Here's how to approach it:

Embrace Fresh Ingredients

Fresh, whole foods should be the stars of your meals. Avoid processed foods that can be laden with hidden sugars and unhealthy fats. Think colorful vegetables, hearty whole grains, and quality protein sources.

Portion Control

Understanding portion sizes is crucial in managing blood sugar levels. This doesn't mean you'll be eating tiny, unsatisfying meals; it's about understanding how much your body needs and recognizing when you're full.

Experiment with Flavors

Who said healthy eating has to be boring? Experimenting with herbs, spices, and different cooking methods can bring excitement and flavor to your meals. For instance, grilling vegetables with a sprinkle of fresh herbs can transform a simple side dish into something extraordinary.

Your Support System

Embarking on this journey doesn't mean you're alone. Your healthcare provider, dietitian, family, and even this cookbook can be part of your support system. Feel free to ask questions, seek guidance, and share your progress with those around you.

Day-by-Day Meal Suggestions

Week 1

Day 1
Breakfast: Spinach and Feta Omelette
Lunch: Grilled Lemon Herb Chicken Breast
Dinner: Baked Herb-Crusted Chicken Thighs
Snack 1: Avocado and Tomato Salad
Snack 2: Celery Sticks with Almond Butter
Day 2
Breakfast: Greek Yogurt with Berries
Lunch: Baked Salmon with Asparagus
Dinner: Shrimp and Vegetable Stir-Fry
Snack 1: Cucumber Slices with Hummus
Snack 2: Apple Slices with Peanut Butter
Day 3
Breakfast: Whole Grain Toast with Avocado
Lunch: Beef Stir-Fry with Broccoli
Dinner: Grilled Pork Chops with Apple Sauce
Snack 1: Cherry Tomatoes with Mozzarella
Snack 2: Walnut and Blueberry Mix
Day 4
Breakfast: Scrambled Tofu with Spinach
Lunch: Stuffed Bell Peppers (Vegetarian)
Dinner: Grilled Vegetable Skewers
Snack 1: Baby Carrots with Greek Yogurt Dip
Snack 2: Fresh Pineapple Slices
Day 5
Breakfast: Quinoa and Roasted Veggie Bowl
Lunch: Lentil Soup
Dinner: Avocado and Chickpea Salad
Snack 1: Fresh Berries with Cottage Cheese
Snack 2: Sliced Orange with Cinnamon
Day 6
Breakfast: Oatmeal with Chopped Nuts and Banana
Lunch: Grilled Fish Tacos with Cabbage Slaw
Dinner: Roasted Turkey with Steamed Broccoli
Snack 1: Edamame with Sea Salt

Snack 2: Grapes and Cheese
Day 7
Breakfast: Smoothie with Spinach, Almond Milk, and Chia Seeds
Lunch: Grilled Portobello Mushrooms with Quinoa Salad
Dinner: Baked Lemon Pepper Tilapia
Snack 1: Celery and Carrot Sticks with Ranch Dressing
Snack 2: Small Pear with Almond Butter

Tips for Success

Start with a Solid Understanding

Research Your Specific Needs: Every person with type 2 diabetes has unique needs. Start by understanding your specific nutritional requirements. Consult with healthcare providers or dietitians who specialize in diabetes to develop a clear understanding of what your body needs.

Educate Yourself about Glycemic Index: Learn about the glycemic index and how different foods can affect your blood sugar levels. It will help you make better-informed decisions about what to eat.

Plan Ahead

Create a Meal Plan: Having a meal plan tailored to your needs will take away daily decision-making stress and help you stick to your diet.

Prepare in Advance: If possible, pre-prepare some meals or components like cutting vegetables. It will make sticking to the plan much easier.

Embrace Whole, Unprocessed Foods

Choose Whole Grains and Fresh Produce: Focus on whole grains, fresh fruits, and vegetables. They provide essential nutrients and are often lower in calories and sugars.

Avoid Processed Items: Limit processed foods, which often contain hidden sugars and unhealthy fats that can negatively impact blood sugar levels.

Monitor and Adjust

Track Your Meals and Reactions: Keep a food diary that includes how particular foods make you feel and how they affect your blood sugar levels. This personalized data can be incredibly valuable in adjusting your diet.

Seek Professional Guidance if Needed: If you notice something off or don't feel well with your diet, don't hesitate to seek professional guidance. Adjustments may be needed, and a healthcare provider can offer personalized advice.

Foster a Supportive Environment
Communicate with Family and Friends: Let those around you know about your dietary needs so they can support you in your journey.
Join Supportive Communities: Consider joining online forums or local groups focused on diabetes-friendly eating. Sharing experiences and gaining support from others in similar situations can be motivating and helpful.

Week 2: Exploring Variety and Balance

The second week of our journey into diabetes-friendly eating is one of exploration and learning. It's about stepping out of comfort zones and embracing the colorful and nutrient-dense spectrum of food that nature offers us. At the same time, it's about understanding the delicate balance that must be maintained to keep blood sugar levels stable. So, what exactly does variety and balance mean in the context of a diabetes-friendly diet, and why are they so crucial?

The Palette of Ingredients
Imagine your plate as a canvas, and the ingredients you choose as the palette of colors you have to paint with. A monochrome painting might have its appeal, but there's a unique joy and satisfaction in creating something full of color, texture, and contrast. Similarly, a meal rich in different types of food not only pleases the eye but provides a range of nutrients that are essential for your well-being.

Embracing Variety: A Symphony of Flavors and Nutrients
Variety as a Nutritional Powerhouse
A varied diet is often compared to a colorful mosaic. Each piece contributes something unique, and together they form a complete picture. Embracing variety is not just about preventing mealtime boredom; it's a powerful tool for nutritional well-being.

When you diversify your ingredients, you inherently include a wider range of vitamins, minerals, and other beneficial compounds. Each food group offers specific nutrients that others may lack. For example, legumes provide plant-based protein and fiber, while citrus fruits are rich in vitamin C. Eating a varied diet ensures that you obtain a comprehensive mix of nutrients.

For individuals with type 2 diabetes, this approach supports overall health by providing the body with the nutritional tools it needs to function optimally. It aids in everything from immune function to energy production, from digestion to cellular repair.

The Sensory Experience

Embracing variety is also about enjoying the sensory experience of eating. Different textures, colors, flavors, and aromas contribute to the pleasure of food. A meal composed of various elements can be more satisfying and enjoyable, making it easier to stick to a healthy eating plan.

Imagine a plate filled with different shades of green from leafy vegetables, the vibrant reds of tomatoes, the earthy browns of whole grains, and the rich colors of fruits like berries or oranges. Each of these colors represents different phytochemicals and antioxidants, each with unique health benefits.

Cultural Exploration

Variety allows for the exploration of different cuisines and cultural traditions. By incorporating dishes from around the world, you not only add excitement to your meals but also benefit from the various ways different cultures approach health and nutrition.

For example, Mediterranean cuisine emphasizes heart-healthy fats, fresh vegetables, and whole grains. Asian cooking often includes nutrient-dense ingredients like tofu, fish, and a variety of vegetables. Exploring these culinary traditions can add a new dimension to your diet.

Flexibility and Adaptation

Embracing variety means having the flexibility to adapt to what's available seasonally and locally. It encourages experimentation and the ability to create meals based on what's fresh, ripe, and at its nutritional peak. This adaptability can lead to more satisfying meals and can even be more cost-effective.

The Role of Glycemic Index

One tool that can be helpful in achieving this balance is understanding the Glycemic Index (GI) of foods. The GI measures how quickly a food raises blood sugar levels. Low GI foods, like whole grains, most fruits, and non-starchy vegetables, release sugar slowly into the blood, providing a steady source of energy.

Using the GI as a guide, you can mix and match foods to create meals that satisfy your taste buds while keeping your blood sugar in check. For instance, pairing a higher GI food with a source of protein or healthy fat can balance the meal and prevent sudden spikes in blood sugar levels.

Day-by-Day Meal Suggestion

Week 2

Day 1
Breakfast: Avocado Toast with Cherry Tomatoes
Lunch: Baked Herb-Crusted Chicken Thighs
Dinner: Beef Stir-Fry with Broccoli
Snack 1: Greek Yogurt with Walnuts and Honey
Snack 2: Sliced Cucumbers with Vinegar and Herbs
Day 2
Breakfast: Scrambled Eggs with Spinach and Feta
Lunch: Shrimp and Vegetable Stir-Fry
Dinner: Grilled Lemon Herb Chicken Breast
Snack 1: Fresh Apple Slices with Cheese
Snack 2: Celery Sticks with Guacamole
Day 3
Breakfast: Berry Almond Smoothie
Lunch: Grilled Vegetable Skewers
Dinner: Baked Salmon with Asparagus
Snack 1: Sliced Pear with Almond Butter
Snack 2: Carrot and Bell Pepper Sticks with Hummus
Day 4
Breakfast: Whole Grain Pancakes with Fresh Strawberries
Lunch: Lentil Soup
Dinner: Grilled Pork Chops with Apple Sauce
Snack 1: Edamame with Chili Flakes
Snack 2: Cottage Cheese with Sliced Kiwi
Day 5
Breakfast: Oatmeal with Blueberries and Chia Seeds
Lunch: Avocado and Chickpea Salad
Dinner: Stuffed Bell Peppers (Vegetarian)
Snack 1: Fresh Orange Slices with Cinnamon
Snack 2: Cherry Tomatoes with Mozzarella
Day 6
Breakfast: Greek Yogurt Parfait with Granola and Mango
Lunch: Grilled Fish Tacos with Cabbage Slaw
Dinner: Roasted Turkey with Green Beans
Snack 1: Small Banana with Peanut Butter
Snack 2: Baked Sweet Potato Fries

Day 7
Breakfast: Smoothie with Kale, Pineapple, and Coconut Water
Lunch: Quinoa and Roasted Veggie Bowl
Dinner: Baked Lemon Pepper Tilapia
Snack 1: Fresh Berries with Whipped Cream
Snack 2: Sliced Peach with Greek Yogurt

Tips for Success

Embrace a Colorful Plate

Incorporate Different Colors: By including various colors of fruits and vegetables, you'll ensure a broader range of nutrients. Each color often represents different vitamins and minerals essential for your health.

Explore New Flavors and Textures: Trying new foods can prevent your meal plan from becoming monotonous. Experimenting with different cuisines can also enhance your culinary skills and enjoyment.

Balance Macronutrients

Understand the Importance of Macronutrients: Carbohydrates, proteins, and fats are the three macronutrients that your body needs. Finding the right balance, especially with carbohydrates, is key for managing blood sugar levels.

Consult with a Nutrition Expert: A professional can help you understand how to balance these macronutrients in your daily diet specifically for your type 2 diabetes.

Utilize Healthy Cooking Techniques

Learn Healthy Cooking Methods: Techniques like grilling, steaming, or baking rather than frying can create delicious meals without adding unnecessary fats.

Invest in Quality Cookware: Having the right tools can make healthy cooking more accessible and enjoyable.

Plan for Snacks and Treats

Choose Nutrient-Dense Snacks: Snacks can be part of a balanced diet. Opt for options rich in nutrients, such as nuts or vegetables with hummus.

Enjoy Treats Mindfully: Deprivation can lead to overindulgence later on. Learn to enjoy treats in moderation and within the context of your dietary needs.

Seek Inspiration and Support

Explore New Recipes: Continually seeking new recipes can keep your meals exciting and enjoyable. Websites, cookbooks, and cooking shows focusing on diabetes-friendly recipes can be a great resource.

Build a Support System: Share your journey with friends, family, or support groups.

They can provide encouragement, join you in trying new recipes, and make the process of exploring variety more enjoyable.

Week 3: Mastering Portion Control

Living with type 2 diabetes requires a comprehensive understanding of diet, not just in terms of what foods are consumed, but how they are consumed. One of the pivotal factors in managing this condition is portion control. Let's delve deeper into this crucial aspect, exploring various dimensions twice as exhaustively.

Understanding the Importance of Portion Control
Portion control is more than a strategy to manage weight; it's a nuanced approach that can significantly affect your overall well-being, especially if you have type 2 diabetes.

The Foundation of Health
Controlling portion sizes is foundational to maintaining health. It helps in creating a balance in the diet, ensuring that you're consuming the right amount of each nutrient. Too much of even a good thing can be harmful, and portion control helps in preventing overeating.

Blood Sugar Management
For people with diabetes, maintaining steady blood sugar levels is paramount. Eating controlled portions helps prevent sudden spikes or drops in blood sugar, leading to better control over diabetes.

Weight Management
Portion control aids in managing weight by ensuring that you're consuming only the calories your body needs. This is particularly important for individuals with type 2 diabetes, as weight management plays a vital role in controlling the condition.

Enhancing Relationship with Food
Practicing portion control doesn't mean deprivation; instead, it encourages a healthier relationship with food. Understanding the right amount to eat promotes mindfulness and appreciation for meals, enhancing overall satisfaction and reducing unhealthy cravings.

Strategies for Mastering Portion Sizes
Understanding what constitutes a serving size and how to control it is at the core of portion management. This section explores various techniques to achieve this mastery.

Learning to Recognize Serving Sizes

Recognizing what constitutes a 'serving' is vital. By comparing servings with everyday objects, you can visualize portion sizes more easily. For example, a serving of meat the size of a deck of cards provides a tangible reference point. Familiarizing oneself with these comparisons helps foster a more intuitive understanding of portions.

Utilizing the Plate Method

The plate method is a visually intuitive guide to achieving a balanced meal with controlled portions. It not only helps in maintaining portions but ensures nutritional balance by encouraging a variety of food groups on the plate.

Mindful Eating Practices

Mindful eating is about fully engaging with the eating experience. By focusing on each bite, its taste, texture, and aroma, mindful eating enables you to recognize satiety cues, preventing overeating. Developing this connection with food enhances the joy of eating while promoting portion control.

Using Smaller Plates and Utensils

A simple yet effective strategy is to use smaller plates and utensils. The same quantity of food appears more on a smaller plate, which can psychologically satisfy the appetite with a smaller portion.

Keeping Track

Writing down what and how much you eat helps in understanding eating patterns and making necessary adjustments. This awareness and control foster an ongoing relationship with portion sizes.

Navigating Challenges

Despite its significance, portion control can be challenging. Here we delve into how to overcome these challenges.

Dining Out

Dining out often means larger portions. Sharing a meal or requesting a take-out box helps in managing portion sizes even when eating away from home.

Avoiding Portion Traps

Being aware of hidden traps, like large beverage servings or complimentary bread baskets, can prevent unintentional overeating.

Emphasizing Progress Over Perfection

Mistakes will happen, and that's okay. Emphasizing progress over perfection, and learning from those mistakes, fosters a healthier relationship with food.

Integrating Portion Control into Your Lifestyle

Making portion control a part of your daily routine is an ongoing process that evolves with time and practice.

Gradual Changes

Start with small, achievable changes and gradually integrate them into your lifestyle. This gradual approach ensures that the changes are sustainable.

Professional Guidance

Including a healthcare provider or dietitian in your journey can provide personalized advice that aligns with your specific needs, enhancing your mastery over portion control.

Day-by-Day Meal Suggestion

Week 3

Day 1
Breakfast: Avocado Toast with Cherry Tomatoes
Lunch: Lentil Soup
Dinner: Grilled Lemon Herb Chicken Breast
Snack 1: Fresh Orange Slices with Cinnamon
Snack 2: Sliced Cucumbers with Vinegar and Herbs
Day 2
Breakfast: Scrambled Eggs with Spinach and Feta
Lunch: Grilled Fish Tacos with Cabbage Slaw
Dinner: Grilled Pork Chops with Apple Sauce
Snack 1: Greek Yogurt with Walnuts and Honey
Snack 2: Cherry Tomatoes with Mozzarella
Day 3
Breakfast: Oatmeal with Blueberries and Chia Seeds
Lunch: Baked Herb-Crusted Chicken Thighs
Dinner: Roasted Turkey with Green Beans
Snack 1: Fresh Berries with Whipped Cream
Snack 2: Sliced Pear with Almond Butter
Day 4
Breakfast: Whole Grain Pancakes with Fresh Strawberries
Lunch: Shrimp and Vegetable Stir-Fry

Dinner: Beef Stir-Fry with Broccoli
Snack 1: Small Banana with Peanut Butter
Snack 2: Edamame with Chili Flakes
Day 5
Breakfast: Greek Yogurt Parfait with Granola and Mango
Lunch: Stuffed Bell Peppers (Vegetarian)
Dinner: Baked Lemon Pepper Tilapia
Snack 1: Sliced Peach with Greek Yogurt
Snack 2: Carrot and Bell Pepper Sticks with Hummus
Day 6
Breakfast: Smoothie with Kale, Pineapple, and Coconut Water
Lunch: Grilled Vegetable Skewers
Dinner: Baked Salmon with Asparagus
Snack 1: Fresh Apple Slices with Cheese
Snack 2: Baked Sweet Potato Fries
Day 7
Breakfast: Berry Almond Smoothie
Lunch: Avocado and Chickpea Salad
Dinner: Quinoa and Roasted Veggie Bowl
Snack 1: Celery Sticks with Guacamole
Snack 2: Cottage Cheese with Sliced Kiwi

Tips for Success

Understand What a Portion Really Is
Learn Standard Portion Sizes: Familiarize yourself with what constitutes a standard portion size for various food groups. Understanding what a portion looks like can prevent unintentional overeating.
Use Tools and Guides: Tools like measuring cups and a food scale can help accurately measure portions, while visual guides can offer comparisons to everyday objects for quick portion size assessments.

Avoid Eating Directly from Packages
Serve Meals on Individual Plates: Pouring or serving food into a bowl or onto a plate helps gauge how much you're consuming, reducing the risk of mindless overeating.
Pre-Portion Snacks: Consider pre-portioning snacks into individual containers. This can help prevent overconsumption and make grab-and-go snacking easier.

Embrace Mindful Eating

Eat Slowly and Chew Well: Taking the time to eat slowly and savor each bite allows your brain to catch up with your stomach, preventing overeating.

Pay Attention to Hunger and Fullness Cues: Learning to recognize when you're hungry or full, and respecting those signals, can play a crucial role in mastering portion control.

Choose the Right Tableware

Use Smaller Plates and Bowls: Smaller dishes can help control portions by making a smaller amount of food look more substantial. This simple visual trick can help you feel more satisfied with less.

Consider Portion-Controlled Dishware: Some plates and bowls are designed with portion control in mind, with marked sections for different food groups, assisting in balanced meal preparation.

Monitor and Adjust as Needed

Keep a Food Diary: Documenting what and how much you eat can provide insight into your eating habits and help identify areas for improvement.

Seek Professional Guidance: A registered dietitian specializing in diabetes care can offer personalized advice on portion control, tailored to your needs, preferences, and medical condition.

Week 4: Building Confidence and Sustainability

The journey towards managing type 2 diabetes through proper nutrition and lifestyle changes is as much about persistence and continuous growth as it is about understanding the basics. Week 4 emphasizes the importance of Building Confidence and Sustainability. This phase is vital, as it reinforces the habits learned and allows them to blossom into a sustainable way of life.

Building Confidence in Your Culinary Skills

Embracing the Learning Curve

Cooking, especially when focusing on specialized dietary needs, can be intimidating at first. It's essential to understand that mistakes, experimentation, and gradual growth are part of the learning curve. Embracing this journey with an open mind builds confidence.

Practicing Regularly

The saying, "practice makes perfect," holds true here. Regularly engaging in cooking and experimenting with new recipes will enhance your comfort in the kitchen.

Seeking Support and Encouragement

Family, friends, and online communities dedicated to diabetic-friendly cooking can offer support and encouragement. Sharing successes and challenges fosters a sense of community, enhancing self-assurance.

Celebrating Achievements

Regardless of how small they might seem, celebrating achievements is crucial. Whether it's mastering a new cooking technique or successfully following a new recipe, acknowledging these milestones fosters confidence.

Sustaining a Diabetes-Friendly Diet

Creating a sustainable diabetes-friendly diet requires understanding, patience, and gradual adaptation. Let's explore how to build this sustainability.

Establishing Routine and Consistency

Consistency is vital in managing type 2 diabetes. Establishing a routine, not just around meals but also shopping and meal planning, creates a stable and manageable pattern.

Flexibility within Boundaries

While routine is crucial, there must also be flexibility within the established boundaries. A diet that's too rigid can lead to burnout, so allowing some variations while still adhering to dietary guidelines maintains engagement and satisfaction.

Integrating Preferences

Sustainability doesn't mean sacrificing taste or preferences. Including favorite flavors and dishes, modified to suit dietary needs, makes the diet more enjoyable and thus more sustainable.

Education and Awareness

Understanding the 'why' behind dietary choices enables you to make informed decisions. Education about how different foods impact diabetes gives you the tools to make choices that align with your health goals.

Building Confidence Outside the Kitchen

Managing diabetes through diet isn't confined to the kitchen. Building confidence in various aspects of daily life contributes to overall success.

Eating Out with Confidence

Being able to navigate restaurant menus and make wise choices builds confidence in maintaining dietary habits outside the home. Asking questions and making special requests when dining out empowers you to stick to your diet without feeling restricted.

Travelling with Assurance
Traveling requires planning and adaptation. Confidence in managing your diet while on the go, whether through packing snacks or knowing what to look for in unfamiliar places, adds another layer of self-assurance.

Handling Social Situations
Social gatherings might pose challenges. Developing strategies to enjoy these occasions without straying from the dietary plan, such as eating beforehand or bringing a suitable dish to share, builds confidence in social settings.

Sustainability as a Lifestyle
Sustainability goes beyond a specific diet; it's a lifestyle choice.

Financial Sustainability
A sustainable diet must also be financially viable. This can include budgeting, understanding where to find quality ingredients at an affordable price, and minimizing waste.

Environmental Considerations
For many, sustainability also means being mindful of the environment. This might involve choosing locally-sourced ingredients, reducing plastic usage, or even growing some herbs or vegetables at home.

Emotional Wellness
Emotional well-being is integral to sustainability. Finding joy in the cooking process, feeling satisfied with meals, and maintaining a positive attitude towards the ongoing journey are all part of building a sustainable lifestyle.

Day-by-Day Meal Suggestion

Week 4

Day 1
Breakfast: Scrambled Eggs with Spinach and Feta
Lunch: Baked Salmon with Asparagus
Dinner: Lentil Soup
Snack 1: Cherry Tomatoes with Mozzarella
Snack 2: Edamame with Chili Flakes

Day 2
Breakfast: Greek Yogurt Parfait with Granola and Mango
Lunch: Grilled Lemon Herb Chicken Breast
Dinner: Shrimp and Vegetable Stir-Fry
Snack 1: Sliced Peach with Greek Yogurt
Snack 2: Carrot and Bell Pepper Sticks with Hummus
Day 3
Breakfast: Avocado Toast with Cherry Tomatoes
Lunch: Grilled Vegetable Skewers
Dinner: Roasted Turkey with Green Beans
Snack 1: Fresh Apple Slices with Cheese
Snack 2: Baked Sweet Potato Fries
Day 4
Breakfast: Whole Grain Pancakes with Fresh Strawberries
Lunch: Beef Stir-Fry with Broccoli
Dinner: Baked Lemon Pepper Tilapia
Snack 1: Sliced Cucumbers with Vinegar and Herbs
Snack 2: Celery Sticks with Guacamole
Day 5
Breakfast: Berry Almond Smoothie
Lunch: Grilled Fish Tacos with Cabbage Slaw
Dinner: Baked Herb-Crusted Chicken Thighs
Snack 1: Fresh Berries with Whipped Cream
Snack 2: Small Banana with Peanut Butter
Day 6
Breakfast: Smoothie with Kale, Pineapple, and Coconut Water
Lunch: Avocado and Chickpea Salad
Dinner: Grilled Pork Chops with Apple Sauce
Snack 1: Sliced Pear with Almond Butter
Snack 2: Fresh Orange Slices with Cinnamon
Day 7
Breakfast: Oatmeal with Blueberries and Chia Seeds
Lunch: Quinoa and Roasted Veggie Bowl
Dinner: Stuffed Bell Peppers (Vegetarian)
Snack 1: Greek Yogurt with Walnuts and Honey
Snack 2: Cottage Cheese with Sliced Kiwi

Tips for Success

Set Realistic Goals and Celebrate Achievements
Emphasize Incremental Progress: Focus on setting attainable and realistic short-term goals. Celebrating small achievements can lead to long-term success and builds confidence in your ability to maintain a diabetes-friendly eating pattern.
Reflect on Successes and Challenges: Regularly take time to reflect on what's working and what could be improved. Acknowledge the progress made and adjust as needed.

Cultivate a Supportive Environment
Engage Family and Friends: Let those close to you know your goals and how they can support you. Cooking together or sharing meal planning responsibilities can build a supportive environment for sustainable change.
Connect with a Community or Group: Finding a community or support group with similar goals can foster encouragement and accountability.

Build a Flexible Meal Plan
Include Favorite Foods: Integrate some of your favorite foods into your meal plan, making necessary adjustments to fit within your dietary needs. This fosters a sense of satisfaction and sustainability.
Learn to Make Adjustments: Life is unpredictable, and having the flexibility to make changes to your meal plan ensures that you can stay on track even when unexpected situations arise.

Invest in Continued Education and Skills Development
Keep Learning: Continued education about diabetes-friendly eating and new recipes will keep your meal plan fresh and exciting. Building skills around cooking, shopping, and meal prep will enhance confidence and enjoyment in the kitchen.
Explore New Culinary Techniques: Experimenting with new cooking techniques and flavors can make meal preparation more engaging and enjoyable, enhancing your confidence in the kitchen.

Emphasize Long-Term Wellness, Not Just Short-Term Goals
Focus on Overall Health and Well-being: Building confidence and sustainability goes beyond merely following a meal plan. Emphasize overall wellness, considering aspects like physical activity, sleep, and stress management.
Consult Healthcare Professionals: Regular check-ins with healthcare providers, including dietitians, can provide ongoing support, personalized adjustments, and encouragement, fostering long-term success in diabetes management.

As we conclude Chapter 3, we reflect on the comprehensive 30-day journey we've just explored together. From the foundational principles of diabetes-friendly eating to the intricate art of portion control, we've unraveled the complexities of managing type 2 diabetes through mindful and joyous eating.

Through exploring variety and balance, we've seen that a diabetes-friendly diet doesn't have to be restrictive. Instead, it invites creativity and pleasure in cooking, allowing you to discover new tastes and textures that nourish your body and soul.

Mastering portion control has hopefully transformed your relationship with food, enabling you to listen to your body and respond to its needs in a loving and sensible way. The tools and insights provided here aim to guide you to a path of continued success.

Building confidence and sustainability is an ongoing process, but one that's integral to lasting success. The strategies discussed offer a roadmap to a fulfilling and sustainable lifestyle that aligns with your health goals without feeling like a burden.

May this chapter serve as an inspiring companion in your continued journey towards health, happiness, and a satisfying culinary adventure. The wisdom, recipes, and daily guidance in these pages are not only tools for a month but resources for a lifetime.

Chapter 4: Recipes

Breakfast Recipes

Smoothies and Drinks

Green Delight Smoothie

Servings: 1 Person
Prep. time: 5 minutes
Ingredients:
1 cup spinach leaves
1 small green apple, cored and sliced
1/2 avocado, pitted
1 cup unsweetened almond milk
A pinch of cinnamon
Ice cubes
Directions:

Place spinach, apple slices, avocado, almond milk, cinnamon, and ice cubes in a blender.
Blend on high until smooth and creamy. Pour into a glass and serve immediately.
Nutr. values:
Calories: 220, Fat: 9g, Protein: 5g, Carbohydrates: 33g, Fiber: 9g, Sugars: 18g

Blueberry Breakfast Shake

Servings: 1 Person
Prep. time: 5 minutes
Ingredients:
1/2 cup blueberries, fresh or frozen
1 scoop protein powder (preferably vanilla or unflavored)
1 cup unsweetened coconut water
1 tablespoon chia seeds
Ice cubes
Directions:
In a blender, combine blueberries, protein powder, coconut water, chia seeds, and ice cubes.
Blend on high speed until the shake is smooth and frothy.
Pour into a chilled glass and enjoy immediately.
Nutr. values:
Calories: 240, Fat: 5g, Protein: 20g, Carbohydrates: 30g, Fiber: 8g, Sugars: 12g

Mocha Morning Drink

Servings: 1 Person
Prep. time: 10 minutes
Ingredients:
1 cup brewed black coffee
1 tablespoon cocoa powder
1 tablespoon sugar-free syrup
2 tablespoons skim milk
Directions:
In a small saucepan, heat the brewed coffee over medium heat.
Add cocoa powder, sugar-free syrup, and skim milk, stirring continuously until well combined.
Pour the mixture into a mug and enjoy hot.
Nutr. values:
Calories: 40, Fat: 0.5g, Protein: 2g, Carbohydrates: 8g, Fiber: 2g, Sugars: 0g

Egg Dishes

Veggie Omelette

Servings: 1 Person
Prep. time: 10 minutes
Ingredients:
2 eggs, beaten
1/4 cup diced bell peppers
1/4 cup diced tomatoes
1/4 cup shredded spinach
Salt and pepper to taste
Directions:
Heat a non-stick skillet over medium heat and lightly grease with cooking spray.
In a bowl, whisk the eggs with salt and pepper.
Pour the beaten eggs into the skillet, tilting to cover the base evenly.
Sprinkle diced bell peppers, tomatoes, and shredded spinach evenly over the eggs.
Cook for 2-3 minutes until the eggs are set but still slightly runny on top.
Carefully fold the omelette in half and cook for another 2 minutes until fully set.
Slide onto a plate and serve hot.
Nutr. values:
Calories: 200, Fat: 12g, Protein: 18g, Carbohydrates: 5g, Fiber: 1g, Sugars: 3g

Avocado Egg Cups

Servings: 1 Person
Prep. time: 15 minutes
Ingredients:
1 avocado, halved and pitted
2 eggs
Salt and pepper to taste
1 tablespoon chopped chives
Directions:

Preheat the oven to 350°F (175°C).
Scoop out some of the flesh from the avocado halves to create enough space for the eggs.
Place the avocado halves in a baking dish.
Crack an egg into each avocado half.
Season with salt and pepper.

Bake for 15 minutes, or until the eggs are cooked to your liking.
Garnish with chopped chives and serve hot.
Nutr. values:
Calories: 360, Fat: 30g, Protein: 14g, Carbohydrates: 15g, Fiber: 11g, Sugars: 2g

Breakfast Egg Muffins

Servings: 1 Person
Prep. time: 25 minutes
Ingredients:
3 eggs, beaten
1/4 cup diced mushrooms
1/4 cup diced ham
1/4 cup grated low-fat cheese
Salt and pepper to taste
Directions:
Preheat the oven to 350°F (175°C) and lightly grease a muffin tin.
In a bowl, whisk the eggs with salt and pepper.
Divide the egg mixture evenly among three muffin cups.
Sprinkle diced mushrooms, ham, and grated cheese over each cup.
Bake for 20 minutes, or until the eggs are set and lightly golden.
Let cool for a few minutes, then carefully remove the muffins from the tin.
Serve warm.
Nutr. values:
Calories: 280, Fat: 18g, Protein: 25g, Carbohydrates: 3g, Fiber: 1g, Sugars: 1g

Whole Grain Options

Quinoa Breakfast Bowl

Servings: 1 Person
Prep. time: 15 minutes
Ingredients:
1/2 cup cooked quinoa
1/4 cup chopped nuts (such as almonds or walnuts)
1/4 cup sliced strawberries
1 tablespoon honey
Directions:
In a bowl, combine the cooked quinoa with the chopped nuts and sliced strawberries.
Drizzle with honey and gently toss to combine.
Serve at room temperature or chilled, as desired.
Nutr. values:
Calories: 350, Fat: 14g, Protein: 9g, Carbohydrates: 48g, Fiber: 6g, Sugars: 18g

Overnight Oats with Almond Milk

Servings: 1 Person
Prep. time: 8 hours (overnight)
Ingredients:
1/2 cup rolled oats
1 cup unsweetened almond milk
1/2 banana, sliced
1 teaspoon vanilla extract
Directions:
In a bowl or jar, combine the rolled oats and unsweetened almond milk.
Cover and refrigerate overnight.
In the morning, stir the oats and add the sliced banana and vanilla extract.
Mix well and enjoy cold.
Nutr. values:
Calories: 280, Fat: 6g, Protein: 8g, Carbohydrates: 50g, Fiber: 8g, Sugars: 10g

Whole Wheat Breakfast Burrito

Servings: 1 Person
Prep. time: 10 minutes
Ingredients:
1 whole wheat tortilla
2 scrambled eggs
1/4 cup cooked black beans, drained and rinsed
1/4 cup salsa

1 tablespoon low-fat sour cream
Directions:
Lay the whole wheat tortilla flat on a clean surface.
Place the scrambled eggs in the center of the tortilla.
Top with black beans, salsa, and a dollop of low-fat sour cream.
Fold the sides of the tortilla over the filling, then roll up from the bottom to encase the ingredients.
Serve immediately, optionally cutting in half for easier eating.
Nutr. values:
Calories: 350, Fat: 12g, Protein: 20g, Carbohydrates: 42g, Fiber: 8g, Sugars: 3g

Multigrain Pancakes with Berries

Servings: 1 Person
Prep. time: 20 minutes
Ingredients:
1/2 cup multigrain pancake mix
1/4 cup skim milk
1 egg, beaten
1/2 cup mixed berries (such as blueberries, raspberries, and strawberries)
Directions:
In a bowl, whisk together the multigrain pancake mix, skim milk, and beaten egg until smooth.
Heat a non-stick skillet over medium heat and lightly grease with cooking spray.
Pour 1/3 of the batter into the skillet and cook for 2-3 minutes, or until bubbles form on the surface.
Flip the pancake and cook for another 2 minutes, or until golden brown.
Repeat with the remaining batter to make 3 pancakes.
Top with mixed berries and serve hot.
Nutr. values:
Calories: 320, Fat: 5g, Protein: 12g, Carbohydrates: 58g, Fiber: 7g, Sugars: 10g

Apple Cinnamon Oatmeal

Servings: 1 Person
Prep. time: 10 minutes
Ingredients:
1/2 cup steel-cut oats
1 small apple, diced
1/2 teaspoon ground cinnamon
1 cup water
Directions:
In a small saucepan, combine the steel-cut oats, diced apple, ground cinnamon, and water.
Bring to a simmer over medium heat, stirring occasionally.
Reduce the heat to low and cover.
Cook for 7-10 minutes, or until the oats are tender and the apple is soft.
Serve hot, optionally garnished with a sprinkle of extra cinnamon.
Nutr. values:
Calories: 250, Fat: 3g, Protein: 7g, Carbohydrates: 51g, Fiber: 8g, Sugars: 15g

Chia Seed and Berry Parfait

Servings: 1 Person
Prep. time: 10 minutes
Ingredients:
2 tablespoons chia seeds
1/2 cup unsweetened almond milk
1/2 cup mixed berries (such as blueberries, raspberries, and strawberries)
1 tablespoon honey
Directions:
In a small bowl, mix the chia seeds with the unsweetened almond milk.

Let sit for 5 minutes, or until the chia seeds have absorbed the liquid and formed a gel-like consistency.

In a glass or jar, layer the chia seed mixture with the mixed berries and honey, repeating the layers until all the ingredients are used.

Serve immediately, or refrigerate for later enjoyment.

Nutr. values:

Calories: 230, Fat: 9g, Protein: 7g, Carbohydrates: 34g, Fiber: 12g, Sugars: 18g

Lunch Recipes

Salads

Spinach and Strawberry Salad

Servings: 1 Person
Prep. time: 10 minutes
Ingredients:
Spinach leaves, 1 cup
Fresh strawberries, 5, halved
Feta cheese, 2 tablespoons
Walnuts, 1 tablespoon
Balsamic vinaigrette, 1 tablespoon
Directions:
Wash the spinach leaves and strawberries.
Place spinach leaves in a bowl.
Add strawberries, feta cheese, and walnuts.
Drizzle balsamic vinaigrette on top.
Toss the salad gently and serve.
Nutr. values:
Calories: 160
Protein: 5g
Carbohydrates: 10g
Fats: 10g

Quinoa and Avocado Salad

Servings: 1 Person
Prep. time: 20 minutes
Ingredients:
Quinoa, ½ cup cooked
Avocado, ½, diced
Cherry tomatoes, 5
Cucumber, ¼, diced
Lime juice, 1 tablespoon
Salt and pepper to taste
Directions:
Cook quinoa according to package instructions and let it cool.
In a bowl, combine quinoa, avocado, cherry tomatoes, and cucumber.
Add lime juice, salt, and pepper.
Toss everything together and serve chilled.
Nutr. values:
Calories: 250
Protein: 8g
Carbohydrates: 30g
Fats: 12g

Grilled Chicken Caesar Salad

Servings: 1 Person
Prep. time: 20 minutes
Ingredients:
Grilled chicken breast, 1, sliced
Romaine lettuce, 1 cup, torn
Croutons, 2 tablespoons
Parmesan cheese, 2 tablespoons
Caesar dressing, 2 tablespoons
Directions:
Toss the lettuce, croutons, and chicken in a bowl.
Sprinkle with Parmesan cheese.
Drizzle Caesar dressing over the top.
Mix well to coat and serve immediately.
Nutr. values:
Calories: 320
Protein: 28g
Carbohydrates: 20g
Fats: 12g

Beetroot and Goat Cheese Salad

Servings: 1 Person
Prep. time: 15 minutes
Ingredients:
Beetroot, 1 medium, roasted and sliced
Goat cheese, 2 tablespoons, crumbled
Arugula, 1 cup
Olive oil, 1 tablespoon
Balsamic vinegar, 1 tablespoon
Salt and pepper to taste
Directions:
In a bowl, place arugula and beetroot slices.
Top with crumbled goat cheese.
In a small bowl, whisk together olive oil, balsamic vinegar, salt, and pepper.
Drizzle the dressing over the salad and serve.
Nutr. values:
Calories: 180
Protein: 7g
Carbohydrates: 15g
Fats: 10g

Tropical Fruit Salad

Servings: 1 Person
Prep. time: 10 minutes
Ingredients:
Mango, ½, diced
Pineapple, 2 slices, diced
Kiwi, 1, diced
Coconut flakes, 1 tablespoon
Lime juice, 1 tablespoon
Directions:
Combine all the diced fruits in a bowl.
Sprinkle with coconut flakes.
Drizzle lime juice over the top.
Gently toss and serve chilled.
Nutr. values:
Calories: 150
Protein: 2g

Carbohydrates: 35g   Fats: 2g

Soups

Tomato Basil Soup

Servings: 1 Person
Prep. time: 20 minutes
Ingredients:
Tomatoes, 2, chopped
Fresh basil leaves, 5
Garlic, 1 clove, minced
Vegetable broth, 1 cup
Salt and pepper to taste
Olive oil, 1 teaspoon
Directions:
In a pot, heat olive oil and sauté garlic until fragrant.

Add tomatoes, basil, and vegetable broth.
Simmer for 15 minutes.
Use an immersion blender or regular blender to puree the soup.
Season with salt and pepper and serve hot.
Nutr. values:
Calories: 90
Protein: 3g
Carbohydrates: 12g
Fats: 4g

Chicken Noodle Soup

Servings: 1 Person
Prep. time: 30 minutes
Ingredients:
Chicken breast, 1, cooked and shredded
Egg noodles, ½ cup, cooked
Carrots, 1, sliced
Celery, 1 stalk, sliced
Chicken broth, 1½ cups
Salt and pepper to taste
Directions:
In a pot, combine chicken, noodles,

carrots, celery, and chicken broth.
Bring to a simmer and cook for 15-20 minutes until vegetables are tender.
Season with salt and pepper and serve hot.
Nutr. values:
Calories: 250
Protein: 25g
Carbohydrates: 25g
Fats: 5g

Lentil Soup

Servings: 1 Person
Prep. time: 40 minutes
Ingredients:
Lentils, ½ cup, rinsed
Carrots, 1, diced
Onions, ½, diced
Garlic, 1 clove, minced
Vegetable broth, 2 cups
Cumin, ½ teaspoon
Salt and pepper to taste
Olive oil, 1 teaspoon
Directions:
In a pot, heat olive oil and sauté onions and garlic until soft.
Add carrots, lentils, cumin, salt, and vegetable broth.
Bring to a boil and then reduce to a simmer, cooking for 30 minutes or until lentils are tender.
Season with salt and pepper and serve hot.
Nutr. values:
Calories: 240
Protein: 16g
Carbohydrates: 40g
Fats: 4g

Butternut Squash Soup

Servings: 1 Person
Prep. time: 30 minutes
Ingredients:
Butternut squash, 1 cup, roasted and pureed
Vegetable broth, 1 cup
Nutmeg, ¼ teaspoon
Salt and pepper to taste
Cream, 1 tablespoon (optional)
Directions:
In a pot, combine butternut squash puree, vegetable broth, and nutmeg.
Bring to a simmer and cook for 10 minutes.
Season with salt and pepper.
Add cream if desired, stir and serve hot.

Nutr. values:
Calories: 110
Protein: 2g
Carbohydrates: 25g
Fats: 2g (without cream)

Spinach and Potato Soup

Servings: 1 Person
Prep. time: 25 minutes
Ingredients:
Spinach, 1 cup, chopped
Potatoes, 1 medium, diced
Onion, ½, chopped
Garlic, 1 clove, minced
Vegetable broth, 1½ cups
Salt and pepper to taste
Olive oil, 1 teaspoon
Directions:
In a pot, heat olive oil and sauté onion and garlic until soft.

Add potatoes, spinach, and vegetable broth.
Bring to a simmer and cook for 15-20 minutes until potatoes are tender.
Use an immersion blender or regular blender to puree the soup.
Season with salt and pepper and serve hot.
Nutr. values:
Calories: 180
Protein: 4g
Carbohydrates: 35g
Fats: 4g

Sandwiches and Wraps

Turkey Avocado Wrap

Servings: 1 Person
Prep. time: 10 minutes
Ingredients:
Whole wheat wrap, 1
Turkey breast, 2 slices
Avocado, ½, sliced
Lettuce, 1 leaf
Tomato, 2 slices
Mustard, 1 teaspoon
Directions:
Lay the whole wheat wrap flat on a surface.

Arrange turkey, avocado, lettuce, and tomato on the wrap.
Drizzle with mustard.
Fold the wrap, tucking in the sides, and roll tightly.
Cut in half and serve.
Nutr. values:
Calories: 350
Protein: 20g
Carbohydrates: 35g
Fats: 15g

Grilled Vegetable Panini

Servings: 1 Person
Prep. time: 15 minutes
Ingredients:
Whole grain bread, 2 slices
Zucchini, ½, thinly sliced
Bell pepper, ½, thinly sliced
Mozzarella cheese, 1 slice
Pesto sauce, 1 tablespoon
Olive oil, 1 teaspoon
Directions:
Heat a grill pan and brush with olive oil.

Grill zucchini and bell pepper until tender.
Spread pesto sauce on one slice of bread.
Layer grilled vegetables and mozzarella cheese on top.
Close with the second slice of bread.
Place the sandwich in a panini press or grill pan, pressing down until toasted and cheese is melted.
Serve hot.

Nutr. values:
Calories: 380
Protein: 18g
Carbohydrates: 40g
Fats: 15g

Tuna Salad Sandwich

Servings: 1 Person
Prep. time: 10 minutes
Ingredients:
Whole grain bread, 2 slices
Canned tuna in water, ½ cup, drained
Mayonnaise, 1 tablespoon
Celery, 1 stalk, chopped
Lettuce, 1 leaf
Salt and pepper to taste
Directions:
In a bowl, combine tuna, mayonnaise, celery, salt, and pepper.
Place the lettuce leaf on one slice of bread.
Spread the tuna salad mixture on top.
Close with the second slice of bread and serve.
Nutr. values:
Calories: 320
Protein: 30g
Carbohydrates: 30g
Fats: 10g

Chicken and Hummus Pita

Servings: 1 Person
Prep. time: 10 minutes
Ingredients:
Whole wheat pita, 1
Chicken breast, 1, cooked and sliced
Hummus, 2 tablespoons
Cucumber, 5 slices
Tomato, 2 slices
Directions:
Cut the pita in half to create a pocket.
Spread hummus inside the pita.
Fill with chicken, cucumber, and tomato slices.
Serve immediately or wrap in foil for a grab-and-go lunch.
Nutr. values:
Calories: 350
Protein: 35g
Carbohydrates: 30g
Fats: 10g

Egg Salad Sandwich

Servings: 1 Person
Prep. time: 15 minutes
Ingredients:
Whole grain bread, 2 slices
Eggs, 2, boiled and chopped
Mayonnaise, 1 tablespoon
Mustard, 1 teaspoon
Salt and pepper to taste
Lettuce, 1 leaf
Directions:
In a bowl, combine chopped eggs, mayonnaise, mustard, salt, and pepper.
Place the lettuce leaf on one slice of bread.
Spread the egg salad mixture on top.
Close with the second slice of bread and serve.
Nutr. values:
Calories: 350
Protein: 20g
Carbohydrates: 30g
Fats: 18g

Dinner Recipes

Poultry

Grilled Lemon Herb Chicken Breast

Servings: 1 Person
Prep. time: 30 minutes
Ingredients: 1 chicken breast, juice of 1 lemon, 1 tsp olive oil, 1 garlic clove minced, 1 tsp thyme, salt, pepper
Directions:
Marinate the chicken breast with lemon juice, olive oil, minced garlic, thyme, salt, and pepper.
Let marinate for at least 15 minutes.
Preheat the grill to medium heat.
Grill the chicken for 5-7 minutes on each side or until fully cooked.
Serve with steamed vegetables.
Nutr. values: Calories 250, Protein 30g, Carbohydrates 4g, Fat 11g

Baked Herb-Crusted Chicken Thighs

Servings: 1 Person
Prep. time: 40 minutes
Ingredients: 1 chicken thigh, 2 tsp whole grain breadcrumbs, 1 tsp rosemary, 1 tsp olive oil, salt, pepper
Directions:
Preheat the oven to 375°F.
Mix breadcrumbs, rosemary, salt, and pepper.
Coat the chicken thigh with olive oil, then dip into breadcrumb mixture.
Place the coated thigh on a baking sheet.
Bake for 25-30 minutes or until cooked through.
Serve with a side salad.
Nutr. values: Calories 270, Protein 25g, Carbohydrates 7g, Fat 15g

Spinach Stuffed Chicken Breast

Servings: 1 Person
Prep. time: 35 minutes
Ingredients: 1 chicken breast, ½ cup spinach, 1 tbsp feta cheese, 1 tsp olive oil, salt, pepper
Directions:
Preheat the oven to 375°F.
Cut a pocket into the chicken breast.
Stuff with spinach and feta cheese.
Secure with toothpicks if necessary.
Season with salt and pepper.
Bake for 25-30 minutes or until cooked through.
Nutr. values: Calories 260, Protein 30g, Carbohydrates 2g, Fat 12g

Turkey Lettuce Wraps

Servings: 1 Person
Prep. time: 20 minutes
Ingredients: 4 oz ground turkey, 1 lettuce leaf, ¼ cup diced tomatoes, ¼ cup diced onions, 1 tsp olive oil, salt, pepper
Directions:
Cook ground turkey in olive oil until browned.
Season with salt and pepper.
Place turkey in lettuce leaf.
Top with diced tomatoes and onions.
Wrap and serve.
Nutr. values: Calories 220, Protein 22g, Carbohydrates 5g, Fat 12g

Chicken and Veggie Stir-Fry

Servings: 1 Person
Prep. time: 25 minutes
Ingredients: 4 oz chicken, ½ cup broccoli, ½ cup bell pepper, 1 tsp olive oil, 1 tsp low-sodium soy sauce, garlic, ginger
Directions:
Heat olive oil in a pan over medium heat.
Add chicken and cook until browned.
Add garlic, ginger, broccoli, and bell pepper.
Stir-fry for 5-7 minutes.
Add soy sauce and cook for another 2 minutes.
Serve hot.
Nutr. values: Calories 230, Protein 25g, Carbohydrates 10g, Fat 8g

Fish and Seafood

Baked Salmon with Asparagus

Servings: 1 Person
Prep. time: 30 minutes
Ingredients: 1 salmon fillet, 5 asparagus spears, 1 tbsp olive oil, lemon zest, salt, pepper
Directions:
Preheat the oven to 375°F.
Place the salmon and asparagus on a baking sheet.
Drizzle with olive oil and sprinkle with lemon zest, salt, and pepper.
Bake for 20 minutes or until salmon is cooked through.
Nutr. values: Calories 310, Protein 34g, Carbohydrates 5g, Fat 17

Shrimp and Vegetable Stir-Fry

Servings: 1 Person
Prep. time: 25 minutes
Ingredients: 5 large shrimp, 1/2 cup broccoli florets, 1/2 carrot sliced, 1/2 bell pepper sliced, 1 tsp olive oil, 1 tsp soy sauce (low sodium), garlic, ginger
Directions:
Heat olive oil in a pan over medium heat.
Add shrimp and cook for 2 minutes each side. Remove and set aside.
In the same pan, sauté garlic and ginger for 1 minute.
Add vegetables and cook for 5-7 minutes until tender.
Return shrimp to pan, add soy sauce, and stir for 2 minutes.
Serve hot.
Nutr. values: Calories 180, Protein 18g, Carbohydrates 10g, Fat 6g

Lemon Garlic Tilapia

Servings: 1 Person
Prep. time: 25 minutes
Ingredients: 1 tilapia fillet, juice of 1 lemon, 1 garlic clove minced, 1 tsp olive oil, salt, pepper
Directions:
Preheat the oven to 375°F.
Place tilapia on a baking sheet.
Mix lemon juice, garlic, olive oil, salt, and pepper.
Pour over tilapia.
Bake for 20 minutes or until cooked through.
Nutr. values: Calories 200, Protein 25g, Carbohydrates 2g, Fat 8g

Grilled Shrimp and Pineapple Skewers

Servings: 1 Person
Prep. time: 20 minutes
Ingredients: 5 large shrimp, 3 pineapple chunks, 1 tsp olive oil, salt, pepper
Directions:
Preheat the grill to medium heat.
Thread shrimp and pineapple onto skewers.
Brush with olive oil, salt, and pepper.
Grill for 3-5 minutes on each side.
Serve with a side salad.
Nutr. values: Calories 180, Protein 15g, Carbohydrates 15g, Fat 6g

Baked Cod with Zucchini Noodles

Servings: 1 Person
Prep. time: 30 minutes
Ingredients: 1 cod fillet, 1 zucchini spiralized, 1 tsp olive oil, salt, pepper, lemon juice
Directions:
Preheat the oven to 375°F.
Season cod with salt, pepper, and lemon juice.
Bake for 20 minutes or until cooked through.
Sauté zucchini noodles in olive oil for 3-5 minutes.
Serve cod over zucchini noodles.
Nutr. values: Calories 200, Protein 25g, Carbohydrates 5g, Fat 8g

Vegetarian

Stuffed Bell Peppers

Servings: 1 Person
Prep. time: 40 minutes
Ingredients: 1 bell pepper, ½ cup cooked quinoa, ¼ cup black beans, ¼ cup corn, ¼ cup diced tomatoes, salt, pepper, 1 tsp olive oil
Directions:
Preheat the oven to 375°F.
Cut the top off the bell pepper and remove the seeds.
In a bowl, mix quinoa, black beans, corn, tomatoes, salt, and pepper.
Stuff the bell pepper with the mixture.
Place in a baking dish and drizzle with olive oil.
Bake for 20 minutes or until the pepper is tender.
Nutr. values: Calories 270, Protein 10g, Carbohydrates 45g, Fat 6g

Grilled Vegetable Skewers

Servings: 1 Person
Prep. time: 30 minutes
Ingredients: 2 cherry tomatoes, 1/2 zucchini sliced, 1/2 bell pepper cut into chunks, 1/2 red onion cut into chunks, 1 tsp olive oil, salt, pepper, herbs
Directions:
Preheat the grill to medium heat.
Thread vegetables onto skewers.
Brush with olive oil, then sprinkle with salt, pepper, and herbs.
Grill for 5-7 minutes on each side or until vegetables are tender.
Serve with a side of whole grain rice.
Nutr. values: Calories 150, Protein 3g, Carbohydrates 25g, Fat 5g

Quinoa and Roasted Veggie Bowl

Servings: 1 Person
Prep. time: 40 minutes
Ingredients: ½ cup cooked quinoa, ½ cup broccoli, ½ cup bell pepper, 1 tsp olive oil, salt, pepper
Directions:
Preheat the oven to 400°F.
Place broccoli and bell pepper on a baking sheet.
Drizzle with olive oil, salt, and pepper.
Roast for 25-30 minutes.
Serve over quinoa.
Nutr. values: Calories 270, Protein 10g, Carbohydrates 45g, Fat 6g

Avocado and Chickpea Salad

Servings: 1 Person
Prep. time: 10 minutes
Ingredients: ½ avocado, ½ cup chickpeas, ¼ cup diced tomatoes, ¼ cup diced cucumbers, lemon juice, salt, pepper
Directions:
In a bowl, combine avocado, chickpeas, tomatoes, and cucumbers.
Drizzle with lemon juice, salt, and pepper.
Mix well and serve.
Nutr. values: Calories 320, Protein 10g, Carbohydrates 35g, Fat 18g

Beef and Pork

Grilled Pork Chops with Apple Sauce

Servings: 1 Person
Prep. time: 30 minutes
Ingredients: 1 pork chop, 1 apple, 1 tsp cinnamon, 1 tsp olive oil, salt, pepper
Directions:
Preheat a grill to medium-high heat.
Season the pork chop with salt and pepper.
Grill for 5-7 minutes on each side or until cooked through.
For the apple sauce, peel and dice the apple.
In a small saucepan, cook the apple with cinnamon until softened.
Mash to create a sauce.
Serve the pork chop with the apple sauce.
Nutr. values: Calories 310, Protein 22g, Carbohydrates 18g, Fat 14g

Beef Stir-Fry with Broccoli

Servings: 1 Person
Prep. time: 25 minutes
Ingredients: 4 oz lean beef sliced, 1 cup broccoli florets, 1/2 onion sliced, 1 tsp olive oil, 1 tsp low-sodium soy sauce, garlic, ginger
Directions:
Heat olive oil in a pan over medium heat.
Add beef and cook for 2 minutes each side. Remove and set aside.
In the same pan, sauté garlic and ginger for 1 minute.
Add broccoli and onion, cook for 5-7 minutes until tender.
Return beef to pan, add soy sauce, and stir for 2 minutes.
Serve hot.
Nutr. values: Calories 280, Protein 25g, Carbohydrates 10g, Fat 14g

Grilled Pork Chops with Green Beans

Servings: 1 Person
Prep. time: 25 minutes
Ingredients: 1 pork chop, ½ cup green beans, 1 tsp olive oil, salt, pepper
Directions:
Preheat the grill to medium heat.
Season pork chop with salt and pepper.
Grill for 6-8 minutes on each side.
Sauté green beans in olive oil for 5-7 minutes.
Serve pork chop with green beans.
Nutr. values: Calories 300, Protein 25g, Carbohydrates 5g, Fat 20g

Beef Stir-Fry with Cauliflower Rice

Servings: 1 Person
Prep. time: 30 minutes
Ingredients: 4 oz beef strips, ½ cup cauliflower rice, ¼ cup bell pepper, ¼ cup snap peas, 1 tsp olive oil, 1 tsp low-sodium soy sauce, garlic, ginger
Directions:
Cook cauliflower rice according to package instructions.
In a pan, heat olive oil over medium heat.
Add beef and cook for 2-3 minutes.
Add garlic, ginger, bell pepper, and snap peas.
Stir-fry for 5-7 minutes.
Add soy sauce and cook for another 2 minutes.
Serve over cauliflower rice.

Nutr. values: Calories 270, Protein 25g, Carbohydrates 10g, Fat 14g

Slow-Cooker Pulled Pork Lettuce Wraps

Servings: 1 Person

Prep. time: 6 hours

Ingredients: 4 oz pork shoulder, 1 lettuce leaf, ¼ cup diced tomatoes, 1 tsp olive oil, salt, pepper

Directions:

Place pork shoulder in a slow cooker. Season with salt and pepper.

Cook on low for 6 hours.
Shred pork with a fork.
Place in a lettuce leaf.
Top with diced tomatoes.
Wrap and serve.

Nutr. values: Calories 220, Protein 22g, Carbohydrates 5g, Fat 12g

Snack and Sides

Vegetable Sides

Garlic Roasted Asparagus

Servings: 1 Person
Prep. time: 15 minutes
Ingredients:
6 asparagus spears
1 garlic clove, minced
1 teaspoon olive oil
Salt and pepper, to taste
Directions:
Preheat the oven to 400°F (200°C). Trim the asparagus spears and place them on a baking tray. In a small bowl, mix together the minced garlic, olive oil, salt, and pepper. Drizzle the mixture over the asparagus and toss to coat evenly. Roast in the oven for 10-12 minutes or until tender. Serve immediately.
Nutr. values:
Calories: 75, Protein: 2.5g, Carbohydrates: 5g, Fat: 5g, Fiber: 2g

Baked Sweet Potato Fries

Servings: 1 Person
Prep. time: 35 minutes
Ingredients:
1 small sweet potato, peeled and cut into fries
1 teaspoon olive oil
Salt and pepper, to taste
Directions:
Preheat the oven to 425°F (220°C). Toss the sweet potato fries with olive oil, salt, and pepper on a baking tray. Bake for 25-30 minutes or until crispy and golden brown, turning halfway through the baking time. Serve hot.
Nutr. values:
Calories: 120, Protein: 2g, Carbohydrates: 26g, Fat: 2g, Fiber: 4g

Sautéed Spinach with Lemon

Servings: 1 Person
Prep. time: 10 minutes
Ingredients:
2 cups fresh spinach
1 teaspoon olive oil
1 tablespoon lemon juice
Salt and pepper, to taste
Directions:
Heat olive oil in a pan over medium heat. Add the fresh spinach and sauté until wilted, about 2-3 minutes. Add lemon juice, salt, and pepper, and stir to combine. Serve immediately.
Nutr. values:
Calories: 50, Protein: 2g, Carbohydrates: 4g, Fat: 3g, Fiber: 2g

Grilled Zucchini with Parmesan

Servings: 1 Person
Prep. time: 15 minutes
Ingredients:
1 small zucchini, sliced
1 teaspoon olive oil
1 tablespoon grated Parmesan cheese
Salt and pepper, to taste
Directions:
Preheat grill to medium-high heat. Toss zucchini slices with olive oil, salt, and pepper. Grill for 3-4 minutes per side or until tender. Sprinkle with grated

Parmesan cheese and serve.
Nutr. values:

Calories: 80, Protein: 4g, Carbohydrates: 4g, Fat: 6g, Fiber: 1g

Steamed Green Beans with Almonds

Servings: 1 Person
Prep. time: 15 minutes
Ingredients:
1 cup green beans, trimmed
1 teaspoon olive oil
1 tablespoon chopped almonds
Salt and pepper, to taste
Directions:
Steam the green beans until tender-crisp, about 5-6 minutes. In a small pan, heat olive oil over medium heat and sauté the chopped almonds until golden brown. Toss the steamed green beans with almonds, salt, and pepper. Serve immediately.
Nutr. values:
Calories: 85, Protein: 3g, Carbohydrates: 7g, Fat: 5g, Fiber: 3g

Grain Sides

Quinoa Salad with Cherry Tomatoes

Servings: 1 Person
Prep. time: 20 minutes
Ingredients:
1/2 cup cooked quinoa
6 cherry tomatoes, halved
1 tablespoon chopped fresh basil
1 teaspoon olive oil
1 teaspoon balsamic vinegar
Salt and pepper, to taste
Directions:
In a bowl, combine the cooked quinoa with cherry tomatoes and fresh basil. In a separate small bowl, whisk together the olive oil, balsamic vinegar, salt, and pepper. Pour the dressing over the quinoa mixture and toss well to coat. Serve chilled or at room temperature.
Nutr. values:
Calories: 175, Protein: 6g, Carbohydrates: 28g, Fat: 5g, Fiber: 3g

Brown Rice with Lemon and Parsley

Servings: 1 Person
Prep. time: 25 minutes
Ingredients:

1/2 cup cooked brown rice
1 teaspoon lemon zest
1 tablespoon chopped fresh parsley
Salt and pepper, to taste
Directions:
In a bowl, mix the cooked brown rice with lemon zest, chopped parsley, salt, and pepper. Stir well to combine and serve hot as a side dish.
Nutr. values:
Calories: 120, Protein: 3g, Carbohydrates: 25g, Fat: 1g, Fiber: 2g

Barley and Mushroom Pilaf

Servings: 1 Person
Prep. time: 40 minutes
Ingredients:
1/2 cup cooked barley
3 button mushrooms, sliced
1 small onion, diced
1 garlic clove, minced
1 teaspoon olive oil
Salt and pepper, to taste
Directions:
Heat olive oil in a pan over medium heat. Sauté the onion and garlic until soft and translucent. Add mushrooms and cook until tender. Stir in cooked

barley, salt, and pepper, and cook for another 2-3 minutes. Serve hot.
Nutr. values:
Calories: 210, Protein: 5g, Carbohydrates: 40g, Fat: 4g, Fiber: 7g

Millet with Sun-dried Tomatoes

Servings: 1 Person
Prep. time: 25 minutes
Ingredients:
1/2 cup cooked millet
2 sun-dried tomatoes, chopped
1 teaspoon olive oil
Salt and pepper, to taste

Directions:
In a bowl, mix the cooked millet with sun-dried tomatoes, olive oil, salt, and pepper. Serve warm as a side dish.
Nutr. values:
Calories: 190, Protein: 6g, Carbohydrates: 35g, Fat: 4g, Fiber: 4g

Wild Rice and Cranberry Salad

Servings: 1 Person
Prep. time: 30 minutes
Ingredients:
1/2 cup cooked wild rice
2 tablespoons dried cranberries
1 tablespoon chopped walnuts
1 teaspoon olive oil
1 teaspoon apple cider vinegar
Salt and pepper, to taste
Directions:
In a bowl, combine the cooked wild rice,

dried cranberries, and chopped walnuts. In a separate small bowl, whisk together the olive oil, apple cider vinegar, salt, and pepper. Pour the dressing over the wild rice mixture and toss well to combine. Serve chilled or at room temperature.
Nutr. values:
Calories: 240, Protein: 5g, Carbohydrates: 45g, Fat: 6g, Fiber: 4g

Snacks

Zucchini and Parmesan Chips

Servings: 1 Person
Prep. time: 30 minutes
Ingredients:
1 medium zucchini, thinly sliced
1 tablespoon grated Parmesan
Olive oil spray
Salt and pepper to taste
Directions:
Preheat the oven to 375°F (190°C). Arrange zucchini slices on a baking

sheet lined with parchment paper. Lightly spray zucchini with olive oil spray and sprinkle with Parmesan, salt, and pepper. Bake for 20-25 minutes until crisp and golden. Let cool and enjoy.
Nutr. values:
Calories: 80, Protein: 6g, Carbohydrates: 5g, Fat: 4g, Fiber: 1g

Almond Butter and Banana Sandwich

Servings: 1 Person
Prep. time: 5 minutes
Ingredients:
1 whole grain bread slice
1 tablespoon almond butter

1/2 banana, sliced
Directions:
Spread almond butter on the bread slice. Arrange banana slices over the almond butter. Cut in half and serve as

a sandwich.
Nutr. values:

Calories: 190, Protein: 6g,
Carbohydrates: 28g, Fat: 8g, Fiber: 4g

Spiced Chickpea Snack

Servings: 1 Person
Prep. time: 40 minutes
Ingredients:
1/2 cup canned chickpeas, drained and rinsed
1 teaspoon olive oil
1/2 teaspoon chili powder
1/2 teaspoon cumin
Salt to taste
Directions:

Preheat the oven to 400°F (200°C). Pat chickpeas dry with a towel. Toss chickpeas with olive oil, chili powder, cumin, and salt. Spread on a baking sheet lined with parchment paper. Bake for 30-35 minutes, stirring occasionally, until crispy. Let cool and enjoy.
Nutr. values:
Calories: 150, Protein: 6g, Carbohydrates: 24g, Fat: 4g, Fiber: 6g

Veggie Sticks with Hummus

Servings: 1 Person
Prep. time: 10 minutes
Ingredients:
1/2 carrot, cut into sticks
1/2 cucumber, cut into sticks
2 tablespoons hummus
Directions:

Place the carrot and cucumber sticks on a plate. Serve with hummus as a dipping sauce.
Nutr. values:
Calories: 100, Protein: 3g, Carbohydrates: 12g, Fat: 4g, Fiber: 3g

Greek Yogurt Berry Parfait

Servings: 1 Person
Prep. time: 5 minutes
Ingredients:
1/2 cup low-fat Greek yogurt
1/4 cup mixed berries (strawberries, blueberries, raspberries)
1 tablespoon chopped nuts (almonds, walnuts)

Directions:
In a glass or bowl, layer Greek yogurt, berries, and nuts. Repeat the layers if desired. Serve chilled.
Nutr. values:
Calories: 150, Protein: 12g, Carbohydrates: 10g, Fat: 6g, Fiber: 2g

Desserts

Fruit-Based Desserts

Baked Cinnamon Apples

Servings: 1 Person
Prep. time: 45 minutes
Ingredients:
1 medium apple, cored and sliced
1 teaspoon cinnamon
1 tablespoon chopped walnuts
Directions:
Preheat the oven to 350°F (175°C).
In a bowl, mix apple slices with cinnamon.
Place the coated apple slices in a baking dish.
Sprinkle with walnuts.
Bake for 35-40 minutes or until the apple is tender.
Serve warm.
Nutr. values:
Calories: 120, Protein: 2g, Carbohydrates: 25g, Fat: 4g, Fiber: 5g

Fresh Berry Salad

Servings: 1 Person
Prep. time: 5 minutes
Ingredients:
1/2 cup mixed berries (strawberries, blueberries, raspberries)
1 teaspoon honey
Mint leaves for garnish
Directions:
In a bowl, combine the mixed berries.
Drizzle honey over the berries.
Gently toss to combine.
Garnish with mint leaves.
Serve chilled.
Nutr. values:
Calories: 60, Protein: 1g, Carbohydrates: 14g, Fat: 0g, Fiber: 3g

Grilled Pineapple with Coconut

Servings: 1 Person
Prep. time: 15 minutes
Ingredients:
2 pineapple slices
1 tablespoon shredded coconut, unsweetened
1 teaspoon honey
Directions:
Preheat a grill or grill pan over medium heat.
Grill pineapple slices for 3-4 minutes on each side or until tender and charred.
Remove from the grill and place on a plate.
Sprinkle with shredded coconut.
Drizzle with honey.
Serve immediately.
Nutr. values:
Calories: 110, Protein: 1g, Carbohydrates: 27g, Fat: 2g, Fiber: 2g

Peach Yogurt Parfait

Servings: 1 Person
Prep. time: 10 minutes
Ingredients:
1/2 peach, sliced
1/2 cup low-fat Greek yogurt
1 tablespoon chopped almonds
Directions:
In a glass or bowl, layer Greek yogurt, peach slices, and almonds.
Repeat the layers if desired.
Serve chilled.
Nutr. values:

Calories: 150, Protein: 12g, Carbohydrates: 15g, Fat: 6g, Fiber: 2g

Chocolate-Dipped Strawberries

Servings: 1 Person

Prep. time: 20 minutes

Ingredients:

3 strawberries

1 ounce dark chocolate (70% cocoa or higher)

1 teaspoon chopped nuts (optional)

Directions:

Melt the dark chocolate in a microwave or over a double boiler.

Dip the strawberries into the melted chocolate, covering half or two-thirds of each strawberry.

Place on a parchment-lined tray.

Sprinkle with chopped nuts if using.

Chill in the refrigerator for at least 10 minutes or until the chocolate has set.

Serve chilled.

Nutr. values:

Calories: 150, Protein: 2g, Carbohydrates: 16g, Fat: 9g, Fiber: 3g

Baked Goods

Almond Flour Blueberry Muffins

Servings: 1 Person
Prep. time: 30 minutes
Ingredients:
1/4 cup almond flour
1 egg
1 tablespoon blueberries
1/2 teaspoon baking powder
1 teaspoon vanilla extract
1 teaspoon honey
Directions:
Preheat the oven to 350°F (175°C).
In a bowl, whisk together the egg, vanilla extract, and honey.
Add the almond flour and baking powder, stirring until combined.
Fold in the blueberries.
Pour the batter into a greased or lined muffin tin.
Bake for 20-25 minutes or until golden brown.
Let cool and serve.
Nutr. values:
Calories: 210, Protein: 9g, Carbohydrates: 12g, Fat: 15g, Fiber: 3g

Baked Apple Oat Bars

Servings: 1 Person
Prep. time: 40 minutes
Ingredients:
1/4 cup rolled oats
1 small apple, diced
1 teaspoon cinnamon
1 tablespoon chopped nuts
1 teaspoon honey
Directions:
Preheat the oven to 350°F (175°C).
In a bowl, mix oats, apple, cinnamon, and nuts.
Add honey and stir until combined.
Press mixture into a greased small baking dish.
Bake for 30 minutes or until golden and set.
Let cool, cut into bars, and serve.
Nutr. values:
Calories: 190, Protein: 4g, Carbohydrates: 31g, Fat: 7g, Fiber: 5g

Sugar-Free Chocolate Brownie

Servings: 1 Person
Prep. time: 30 minutes
Ingredients:
1/4 cup almond flour
1 tablespoon unsweetened cocoa powder
1 egg
1 teaspoon vanilla extract
1 tablespoon melted coconut oil
2 tablespoons stevia
Directions:
Preheat the oven to 350°F (175°C).
In a bowl, mix almond flour, cocoa powder, egg, vanilla extract, coconut oil, and stevia.
Pour the mixture into a greased small baking dish.
Bake for 15-20 minutes or until set.
Let cool, cut into squares, and serve.
Nutr. values:
Calories: 250, Protein: 8g, Carbohydrates: 10g, Fat: 22g, Fiber: 4g

Pumpkin Spice Cookies

Servings: 1 Person
Prep. time: 25 minutes
Ingredients:
1/4 cup canned pumpkin puree
1/4 cup almond flour
1 teaspoon pumpkin spice
1 tablespoon chopped pecans
1 teaspoon honey
Directions:
Preheat the oven to 350°F (175°C).
In a bowl, combine pumpkin puree, almond flour, pumpkin spice, and honey.
Stir in pecans.
Drop spoonfuls onto a lined baking sheet.
Bake for 12-15 minutes or until firm.
Let cool and serve.
Nutr. values:
Calories: 200, Protein: 6g,
Carbohydrates: 14g, Fat: 16g, Fiber: 3g

Lemon Chia Seed Cake

Servings: 1 Person
Prep. time: 40 minutes
Ingredients:
1/4 cup almond flour
1 tablespoon chia seeds
1 teaspoon lemon zest
1 tablespoon lemon juice
1 egg
1 tablespoon stevia
Directions:
Preheat the oven to 350°F (175°C).
In a bowl, whisk the egg, lemon zest, lemon juice, and stevia.
Add the almond flour and chia seeds, stirring until combined.
Pour the batter into a greased or lined

small cake pan.
Bake for 25-30 minutes or until golden and a toothpick inserted comes out clean.
Let cool and serve.

Nutr. values:
Calories: 230, Protein: 9g,
Carbohydrates: 11g, Fat: 18g, Fiber: 4g

No-Sugar-Added-Treats

Avocado Chocolate Pudding

Servings: 1 Person
Prep. time: 10 minutes
Ingredients:
1/2 ripe avocado
2 tablespoons unsweetened cocoa powder
1/2 teaspoon vanilla extract
Stevia to taste
Directions:
Peel and pit the avocado.
In a blender, combine the avocado, cocoa powder, vanilla extract, and stevia.
Blend until smooth and creamy, adding water if needed.
Refrigerate for at least 1 hour or until chilled.
Serve cold.
Nutr. values:
Calories: 170, Protein: 3g, Carbohydrates: 13g, Fat: 14g, Fiber: 7g

Berry Yogurt Parfait

Servings: 1 Person
Prep. time: 5 minutes
Ingredients:
1/2 cup Greek yogurt, unsweetened
1/2 cup mixed berries
1 tablespoon chopped nuts
1/2 teaspoon vanilla extract
Directions:
In a glass, layer the Greek yogurt and mixed berries.
Sprinkle with chopped nuts.
Drizzle with vanilla extract.
Serve immediately or refrigerate until ready to eat.
Nutr. values:
Calories: 150, Protein: 12g, Carbohydrates: 11g, Fat: 6g, Fiber: 2g

Chocolate-Dipped Strawberries

Servings: 1 Person
Prep. time: 15 minutes
Ingredients:
5 fresh strawberries
2 tablespoons sugar-free dark chocolate
1/2 teaspoon coconut oil
Directions:
Wash and dry the strawberries.
Melt the sugar-free chocolate with coconut oil in a heatproof bowl over simmering water.
Dip each strawberry into the melted chocolate, covering half or more.
Place on a parchment-lined tray.
Chill in the refrigerator until the chocolate hardens.
Serve cold.
Nutr. values:
Calories: 140, Protein: 2g, Carbohydrates: 10g, Fat: 10g, Fiber: 2g

Almond Butter Banana Ice Cream

Servings: 1 Person
Prep. time: 10 minutes (plus freezing)
Ingredients:
1 banana, frozen
1 tablespoon almond butter
1/2 teaspoon vanilla extract
Directions:
In a food processor, combine the frozen

banana, almond butter, and vanilla extract.

Process until smooth and creamy, resembling ice cream.

Serve immediately or freeze for later.

Nutr. values:

Calories: 200, Protein: 5g, Carbohydrates: 25g, Fat: 11g, Fiber: 4g

Cinnamon Roasted Nuts

Servings: 1 Person
Prep. time: 20 minutes
Ingredients:
1/4 cup mixed nuts
1/2 teaspoon ground cinnamon
A pinch of salt
Directions:
Preheat the oven to 350°F (175°C).
In a bowl, toss the nuts with cinnamon and salt.

Spread the nuts on a parchment-lined baking sheet.

Bake for 10-15 minutes or until fragrant and golden.

Allow to cool before serving.

Nutr. values:

Calories: 200, Protein: 5g, Carbohydrates: 7g, Fat: 18g, Fiber: 3g

Chapter 5: Special Section

Quick and Easy Recipes: For Busy Days

Quick Avocado Tuna Salad

Servings: 1 Person
Prep. time: 10 minutes
Ingredients:
1 can of tuna, drained
1 ripe avocado, diced
1 tablespoon of olive oil
Salt and pepper to taste
A handful of cherry tomatoes, halved
1 tablespoon of lemon juice
Directions:
In a bowl, mix the drained tuna, diced avocado, olive oil, salt, and pepper.
Add cherry tomatoes and lemon juice and toss until well combined.
Serve chilled or at room temperature.
Nutr. values:
Calories: 400
Protein: 25g
Carbs: 15g
Fat: 28g
Fiber: 9g

Spiced Chicken Wrap

Servings: 1 Person
Prep. time: 15 minutes
Ingredients:
1 chicken breast, cooked and shredded
1 whole-grain tortilla
1/2 cup of lettuce, shredded
2 tablespoons of Greek yogurt
1 teaspoon of paprika
Salt and pepper to taste
Directions:
Mix shredded chicken with paprika, salt, and pepper.
Lay the whole-grain tortilla flat and add the lettuce.
Add the spiced chicken on top of the lettuce.
Dollop the Greek yogurt on top of the chicken.
Roll the tortilla tightly, cut in half, and serve.
Nutr. values:
Calories: 350
Protein: 30g
Carbs: 30g
Fat: 10g
Fiber: 5g

Zesty Shrimp Salad

Servings: 1 Person
Prep. time: 15 minutes
Ingredients:
5 large shrimp, cooked and peeled
1 cup of mixed salad greens
1/2 orange, peeled and segmented
1 tablespoon of vinaigrette dressing
Directions:
In a salad bowl, combine salad greens, orange segments, and shrimp.
Drizzle with vinaigrette dressing and toss to coat.
Serve immediately.
Nutr. values:
Calories: 200
Protein: 15g
Carbs: 18g
Fat: 7g
Fiber: 3g

Turkey and Veggie Stuffed Pita

Servings: 1 Person
Prep. time: 10 minutes
Ingredients:
1 whole-grain pita pocket
3 slices of turkey breast
1/2 cup of mixed bell peppers, sliced
1/4 cup of cucumber, sliced
1 tablespoon of low-fat mayonnaise
Directions:
Cut the pita pocket in half.
Spread the low-fat mayonnaise inside the pita.
Stuff with turkey slices, bell peppers, and cucumber.
Serve immediately or wrap for later.
Nutr. values:
Calories: 300
Protein: 25g
Carbs: 35g
Fat: 7g
Fiber: 5g

Microwave Veggie Omelette

Servings: 1 Person
Prep. time: 5 minutes
Ingredients:
2 eggs, beaten
1/4 cup of bell peppers, diced
1/4 cup of mushrooms, sliced
Salt and pepper to taste
A sprinkle of shredded cheese (optional)
Directions:
In a microwave-safe bowl, combine the beaten eggs, bell peppers, mushrooms, salt, and pepper.
Microwave on high for 2 minutes, or until eggs are fully cooked.
Sprinkle with cheese, if desired, and microwave for an additional 30 seconds.
Serve hot.
Nutr. values:
Calories: 200
Protein: 18g
Carbs: 6g
Fat: 12g
Fiber: 1g

Vegetarian and Vegan Recipes: Plant-Based Options

Spinach and Mushroom Stuffed Eggplant

Servings: 1 Person
Prep. time: 30 minutes
Ingredients:
1 medium eggplant
1 cup spinach, chopped
1/2 cup mushrooms, diced
2 tablespoons olive oil
Salt and pepper to taste
Directions:
Preheat the oven to 400°F (200°C).
Cut the eggplant in half lengthwise and scoop out the flesh, leaving a shell.
In a pan, heat olive oil and sauté spinach and mushrooms until soft.
Fill the eggplant shells with the sautéed vegetables.
Season with salt and pepper.
Bake for 20 minutes or until eggplant is tender.
Serve hot.
Nutr. values:
Calories: 250
Protein: 5g
Carbs: 30g
Fat: 14g
Fiber: 10g

Cauliflower Rice Stir-Fry

Servings: 1 Person
Prep. time: 20 minutes
Ingredients:
1 cup cauliflower rice
1/2 cup mixed vegetables (carrots, peas, bell peppers)
2 tablespoons soy sauce (low-sodium)
1 tablespoon sesame oil
Directions:
Heat sesame oil in a pan.
Add mixed vegetables and sauté until tender.
Add cauliflower rice and cook for 5 minutes, stirring frequently.
Stir in soy sauce and cook for another 2 minutes.
Serve hot.
Nutr. values:
Calories: 180
Protein: 6g
Carbs: 20g
Fat: 10g
Fiber: 5g

Vegan Zucchini Noodles with Pesto

Servings: 1 Person
Prep. time: 15 minutes
Ingredients:
1 medium zucchini, spiralized
1/4 cup vegan pesto
Cherry tomatoes, halved
Salt and pepper to taste
Directions:
In a pan, cook the zucchini noodles for 3-4 minutes.
Add vegan pesto and cherry tomatoes.
Toss until well combined.
Season with salt and pepper.
Serve hot or chilled.
Nutr. values:
Calories: 220
Protein: 4g
Carbs: 15g
Fat: 18g
Fiber: 4g

Chilled Cucumber Soup

Servings: 1 Person
Prep. time: 10 minutes
Ingredients:
1 cucumber, peeled and diced
1 cup almond milk (unsweetened)
Fresh dill
Salt and pepper to taste
Directions:
Blend cucumber, almond milk, and dill until smooth.
Season with salt and pepper.
Chill in the refrigerator for at least 1 hour.
Serve cold.
Nutr. values:
Calories: 100
Protein: 2g
Carbs: 12g
Fat: 5g
Fiber: 2g

Baked Tofu with Broccoli

Servings: 1 Person
Prep. time: 30 minutes
Ingredients:
1/2 block of tofu, cubed
1 cup broccoli florets
1 tablespoon olive oil
2 tablespoons low-sodium soy sauce
Directions:
Preheat the oven to 400°F (200°C).
Toss tofu and broccoli in olive oil and soy sauce.
Spread on a baking sheet.
Bake for 20-25 minutes, flipping halfway through.

Serve hot.
Nutr. values:
Calories: 250
Protein: 18g
Carbs: 15g
Fat: 15g
Fiber: 4g

Spicy Chickpea Curry

Servings: 1 Person
Prep. time: 30 minutes
Ingredients:
1/2 cup chickpeas, cooked
1/2 cup tomatoes, diced
1/4 cup coconut milk
1 teaspoon curry powder
1 teaspoon chili powder
Salt to taste
Directions:
In a pan, simmer tomatoes until soft.
Add chickpeas, coconut milk, curry powder, and chili powder.
Cook for 20 minutes until thickened.
Season with salt.
Serve hot with cauliflower rice.
Nutr. values:
Calories: 300
Protein: 10g
Carbs: 35g
Fat: 15g
Fiber: 8g

Vegan Pancakes with Berry Compote

Servings: 1 Person
Prep. time: 15 minutes
Ingredients:
1/2 cup oat flour
1/2 banana, mashed
1/4 cup almond milk
1/2 cup mixed berries
Directions:
In a bowl, combine oat flour, mashed banana, and almond milk to make the pancake batter.
Cook pancakes on a non-stick pan until golden brown.
Simmer mixed berries in a saucepan until soft to create a compote.
Serve pancakes with berry compote.
Nutr. values:
Calories: 250
Protein: 5g
Carbs: 45g
Fat: 5g
Fiber: 7g

Grilled Portobello Mushrooms with Asparagus

Servings: 1 Person
Prep. time: 15 minutes
Ingredients:
2 large portobello mushrooms
6 asparagus spears
1 tablespoon olive oil
Salt and pepper to taste
Directions:
Preheat a grill or grill pan.
Brush mushrooms and asparagus with olive oil.
Grill for 5-7 minutes on each side until tender.
Season with salt and pepper.
Serve hot.
Nutr. values:
Calories: 150
Protein: 5g
Carbs: 10g
Fat: 10g
Fiber: 4g

Baked Sweet Potato with Avocado

Servings: 1 Person
Prep. time: 45 minutes
Ingredients:
1 medium sweet potato
1/2 avocado, mashed
Salt and pepper to taste
Directions:
Preheat the oven to 400°F (200°C).
Bake sweet potato for 40-45 minutes or until tender.
Cut open and fill with mashed avocado.
Season with salt and pepper.
Serve hot.
Nutr. values:
Calories: 300
Protein: 4g
Carbs: 45g
Fat: 14g
Fiber: 10g

Vegan Creamy Tomato Pasta

Servings: 1 Person
Prep. time: 20 minutes
Ingredients:
1 cup whole-grain pasta, cooked
1/2 cup tomatoes, diced
1/4 cup coconut cream
2 garlic cloves, minced
Salt and pepper to taste
Directions:
In a pan, sauté garlic and tomatoes until soft.
Add coconut cream and simmer for 5 minutes.
Toss in cooked pasta and cook for another 2 minutes.
Season with salt and pepper.
Serve hot.
Nutr. values:
Calories: 350
Protein: 8g
Carbs: 50g
Fat: 15g
Fiber: 8g

Low-Carb Recipes: For Carb Counters

Almond-Crusted Salmon

Servings: 1 Person
Prep. time: 25 minutes
Ingredients:
1 salmon fillet
1/4 cup almond meal
1 teaspoon olive oil
Salt and pepper to taste
Directions:
Preheat the oven to 375°F (190°C).
Mix almond meal, salt, and pepper.
Brush salmon with olive oil and coat with almond mixture.
Bake for 20 minutes or until flaky.
Serve hot with steamed vegetables.
Nutr. values:
Calories: 320
Protein: 35g
Carbs: 4g
Fat: 18g
Fiber: 2g

Zesty Lemon Garlic Shrimp

Servings: 1 Person
Prep. time: 15 minutes
Ingredients:
6 large shrimp, peeled
1 garlic clove, minced
1 tablespoon lemon juice
Salt and pepper to taste
Directions:
Heat olive oil in a pan.
Sauté garlic until fragrant.
Add shrimp, lemon juice, salt, and pepper.
Cook until shrimp are pink.
Serve hot over a bed of spinach.
Nutr. values:
Calories: 160
Protein: 24g
Carbs: 2g
Fat: 6g
Fiber: 0g

Grilled Chicken with Herbed Green Beans

Servings: 1 Person
Prep. time: 20 minutes
Ingredients:
1 chicken breast
1 cup green beans
1 teaspoon mixed herbs (thyme, rosemary)
Salt and pepper to taste
Directions:
Grill chicken until cooked through.
Steam green beans.
Toss green beans with herbs, salt, and pepper.
Serve chicken with herbed green beans.
Nutr. values:
Calories: 270
Protein: 30g
Carbs: 8g
Fat: 12g
Fiber: 4g

Roasted Asparagus with Poached Egg

Servings: 1 Person
Prep. time: 15 minutes
Ingredients:
6 asparagus spears
1 egg
1 teaspoon olive oil
Salt and pepper to taste
Directions:
Preheat the oven to 400°F (200°C).
Toss asparagus with olive oil, salt, and pepper.
Roast for 10 minutes.
Poach egg to desired doneness.
Serve asparagus with poached egg on

top.
Nutr. values:
Calories: 160
Protein: 10g
Carbs: 5g
Fat: 12g
Fiber: 2g

Balsamic-Glazed Brussels Sprouts with Turkey Bacon

Servings: 1 Person
Prep. time: 25 minutes
Ingredients:
1 cup Brussels sprouts, halved
2 slices turkey bacon, chopped
1 tablespoon balsamic vinegar
Salt and pepper to taste
Directions:
In a pan, cook turkey bacon until crispy.
Add Brussels sprouts and sauté.
Drizzle balsamic vinegar, salt, and pepper.
Cook until sprouts are tender.
Serve hot.
Nutr. values:
Calories: 200
Protein: 18g
Carbs: 10g
Fat: 10g
Fiber: 4g

Tofu Stir-Fry with Broccoli

Servings: 1 Person
Prep. time: 15 minutes
Ingredients:
1/2 block tofu, cubed
1 cup broccoli florets
1 tablespoon soy sauce (low-sodium)
1 teaspoon sesame oil
Directions:
Heat sesame oil in a pan.
Add tofu and broccoli, cook until browned.
Stir in soy sauce and cook for 2 minutes.
Serve hot.
Nutr. values:
Calories: 180
Protein: 18g
Carbs: 8g
Fat: 9g
Fiber: 3g

Stuffed Avocado with Tuna Salad

Servings: 1 Person
Prep. time: 10 minutes
Ingredients:
1 avocado, halved
1/2 can tuna, drained
1 tablespoon mayonnaise (sugar-free)
Salt and pepper to taste
Directions:
Mix tuna, mayonnaise, salt, and pepper.
Spoon tuna salad into avocado halves.
Serve chilled.
Nutr. values:
Calories: 320
Protein: 18g
Carbs: 12g
Fat: 26g
Fiber: 8g

Cauliflower Rice with Grilled Chicken

Servings: 1 Person
Prep. time: 20 minutes
Ingredients:
1 chicken breast
1 cup cauliflower rice
Salt and pepper to taste
Directions:
Grill chicken until cooked through.
Sauté cauliflower rice until tender.
Season with salt and pepper.

Serve chicken with cauliflower rice.
Nutr. values:
Calories: 280
Protein: 30g

Carbs: 10g
Fat: 12g
Fiber: 4g

Grilled Eggplant with Herbed Ricotta

Servings: 1 Person
Prep. time: 15 minutes
Ingredients:
1 eggplant, sliced
1/4 cup ricotta cheese
1 teaspoon mixed herbs (basil, oregano)
Salt and pepper to taste
Directions:
Grill eggplant slices until tender.

Mix ricotta with herbs, salt, and pepper.
Spoon ricotta mixture onto eggplant slices.
Serve warm.
Nutr. values:
Calories: 160
Protein: 8g
Carbs: 12g
Fat: 10g
Fiber: 5g

Cucumber and Smoked Salmon Rolls

Servings: 1 Person
Prep. time: 10 minutes
Ingredients:
1 cucumber, sliced lengthwise
4 slices smoked salmon
1 tablespoon cream cheese
Salt and pepper to taste
Directions:
Spread cream cheese on cucumber slices.

Place smoked salmon on top.
Roll up and secure with a toothpick.
Serve chilled.
Nutr. values:
Calories: 180
Protein: 18g
Carbs: 4g
Fat: 10g
Fiber: 1g

High-Fiber Recipes: For Optimal Digestive Health

Chia Berry Pudding

Servings: 1 Person
Prep. time: 5 minutes (plus chilling)
Ingredients:
2 tablespoons chia seeds
1 cup unsweetened almond milk
1/2 cup mixed berries
1 teaspoon vanilla extract
Directions:
Mix chia seeds, almond milk, and vanilla in a bowl.

Cover and chill for at least 2 hours or until thickened.
Top with mixed berries and serve chilled.
Nutr. values:
Calories: 200
Protein: 6g
Carbs: 18g
Fat: 10g
Fiber: 12g

Lentil Spinach Soup

Servings: 1 Person
Prep. time: 30 minutes
Ingredients:

1/2 cup lentils
1 cup spinach
1 garlic clove, minced

Salt and pepper to taste

Directions:
Cook lentils according to package instructions.
Sauté garlic in a pan.
Add spinach and cook until wilted.
Combine lentils and spinach, season with salt and pepper.

Serve hot.

Nutr. values:
Calories: 250
Protein: 18g
Carbs: 40g
Fat: 1g
Fiber: 16g

Whole Grain Penne with Roasted Vegetables

Servings: 1 Person
Prep. time: 25 minutes
Ingredients:
1 cup whole grain penne
1/2 cup cherry tomatoes, halved
1/2 zucchini, sliced
1 teaspoon olive oil
Salt and pepper to taste
Directions:
Cook penne according to package instructions.

Roast tomatoes and zucchini in olive oil until tender.
Toss penne with roasted vegetables.
Season with salt and pepper and serve.

Nutr. values:
Calories: 320
Protein: 10g
Carbs: 60g
Fat: 5g
Fiber: 10g

Apple Walnut Oatmeal

Servings: 1 Person
Prep. time: 15 minutes
Ingredients:
1/2 cup rolled oats
1 apple, chopped
1 tablespoon walnuts, chopped
1 cup water
Directions:
Cook oats in water until soft.

Stir in apple and walnuts.
Serve warm.

Nutr. values:
Calories: 280
Protein: 6g
Carbs: 45g
Fat: 10g
Fiber: 8g

Baked Sweet Potato with Black Beans

Servings: 1 Person
Prep. time: 45 minutes
Ingredients:
1 medium sweet potato
1/2 cup black beans, cooked
Salt and pepper to taste
Directions:
Bake sweet potato at 400°F (200°C) until tender.

Slice open and fill with black beans.
Season with salt and pepper and serve.

Nutr. values:
Calories: 300
Protein: 10g
Carbs: 65g
Fat: 1g
Fiber: 13g

Avocado and Tomato Salad

Servings: 1 Person
Prep. time: 10 minutes
Ingredients:
1 avocado, diced
1 tomato, diced
1 teaspoon olive oil
Salt and pepper to taste
Directions:
Mix avocado and tomato in a bowl.
Drizzle with olive oil and season with salt and pepper.
Serve chilled.
Nutr. values:
Calories: 320
Protein: 4g
Carbs: 20g
Fat: 28g
Fiber: 10g

Broccoli and Almond Stir-Fry

Servings: 1 Person
Prep. time: 15 minutes
Ingredients:
1 cup broccoli florets
1 tablespoon almonds, sliced
1 teaspoon sesame oil
Salt and pepper to taste
Directions:
Heat sesame oil in a pan.
Sauté broccoli until tender.
Add almonds, salt, and pepper.
Cook for 2 more minutes and serve hot.
Nutr. values:
Calories: 180
Protein: 6g
Carbs: 12g
Fat: 14g
Fiber: 5g

Pear and Arugula Salad with Feta

Servings: 1 Person
Prep. time: 10 minutes
Ingredients:
1 pear, sliced
1 cup arugula
1 tablespoon feta cheese, crumbled
1 teaspoon balsamic vinegar
Directions:
Mix pear, arugula, and feta in a bowl.
Drizzle with balsamic vinegar and serve chilled.
Nutr. values:
Calories: 170
Protein: 4g
Carbs: 30g
Fat: 4g
Fiber: 6g

Grilled Portobello Mushrooms

Servings: 1 Person
Prep. time: 15 minutes
Ingredients:
2 large Portobello mushrooms
1 teaspoon olive oil
Salt and pepper to taste
Directions:
Brush mushrooms with olive oil.
Grill until tender, season with salt and pepper.
Serve hot.
Nutr. values:
Calories: 120
Protein: 4g
Carbs: 10g
Fat: 8g
Fiber: 4g

Spaghetti Squash with Pesto

Servings: 1 Person
Prep. time: 40 minutes
Ingredients:
1/2 spaghetti squash
1 tablespoon pesto sauce
Salt and pepper to taste
Directions:
Bake spaghetti squash at 375°F (190°C) until tender.

Scrape out flesh with a fork to create "spaghetti."
Toss with pesto sauce and serve warm.
Nutr. values:
Calories: 140
Protein: 2g
Carbs: 20g
Fat: 7g
Fiber: 4g

Chapter 6: Beyond the Kitchen

Living with type 2 diabetes is about so much more than merely adhering to a specialized diet or taking prescribed medications. While these aspects are crucial, managing diabetes successfully reaches beyond the confines of the kitchen and into various other realms of daily life. In Chapter 6, titled "Beyond the Kitchen," we explore how an integrated and holistic approach towards diabetes can enable you to thrive, not just survive.

Diabetes management isn't just about numbers or measurements, pills, or pricks; it's about adopting a lifestyle that fosters a harmonious balance between different aspects of life. It's about understanding your body and its unique needs and responses. It's about empowering yourself with knowledge, tools, and techniques to navigate daily life with grace and determination.

In this chapter, we'll explore essential topics such as physical activity, stress management, regular health check-ups, and mindful eating. These aren't isolated subjects but are interconnected pieces of a puzzle that, when put together, can offer a comprehensive strategy for a life well-lived with diabetes.

1. **Physical Activity and Diabetes Management**: Exercise isn't just about losing weight or building muscles; it's a vital part of maintaining good blood sugar control. It's about finding activities that you enjoy and making them a regular part of your routine. It's about understanding how your body reacts to different types of exercises and how to adjust your food and medications accordingly.

2. **Stress Management and Mindful Eating**: Our relationship with food goes beyond nutrition. Eating is an emotional experience, and understanding this relationship can lead to a more balanced lifestyle. Managing stress through mindfulness can not only improve mental well-being but can also have a positive impact on your blood sugar levels.

3. **Regular Health Check-ups and Monitoring Blood Sugar Levels**: These practices go hand in hand. Regular check-ups with healthcare professionals ensure that you are on the right track and help in early detection of potential complications. Monitoring your blood sugar levels at home empowers you to make daily decisions that keep you in control.

As we delve into these topics, remember that they are not merely instructions or guidelines; they are pathways to a more fulfilling, healthy, and empowered life. Let's journey together as we go beyond the kitchen and into a world where managing diabetes is not a struggle but a way of life.

Physical Activity and Diabetes Management: Exercise Tips and Guidelines

Physical activity, often regarded as merely an accessory to health, actually plays a central role in managing type 2 diabetes. It's not just about what you eat, but how you move, and the relationship between these two aspects can significantly influence your health journey.

Embracing Physical Activity as a Partner in Health

When we think about physical activity, we often imagine strenuous workouts that demand immense dedication. However, the truth is more nuanced and encouraging. Regular physical exercise can significantly improve insulin sensitivity and help control blood sugar levels, even if it's as simple as walking or stretching.

But where do you start, and how can you make physical activity a joyful part of your routine rather than a burdensome task? Let's explore.

Understanding the Benefits of Exercise

Exercise isn't just about losing weight or building muscles; it's about enhancing overall health. As you engage in regular physical activity, you're likely to see improvements in various aspects of well-being, including emotional balance and heart health.

This broader perspective of exercise can fuel motivation, knowing that each step, stretch, or dance move contributes to a healthier, happier you.

Starting Small and Building Gradually

If exercise is a new frontier for you, it's perfectly fine to start small. Take a walk around your neighborhood or engage in light stretching. Emphasize consistency over intensity at the beginning. Small, manageable activities can build a foundation that allows for more adventurous explorations later on.

The beauty of starting small is that it doesn't feel overwhelming. Over time, as your comfort and capability grow, you can gradually increase the intensity and variety of your workouts, developing a lifelong habit that's rooted in joy rather than obligation.

Finding What You Love

Exercise doesn't have to be dull or monotonous. The world of physical activity is rich with options, from dancing and swimming to biking and hiking. How can you find something that resonates with you?

Exploring Different Options

The best exercise for you is the one you enjoy. Experimenting with different physical activities can make the process enjoyable and inspiring. Try a dance class, or go hiking with friends. When you connect with an activity that you love, it's easier to make it a part of your daily life.

Joining a Community

Sometimes, doing things together can make them more enjoyable. Consider joining a local sports team or dance class. Connecting with others through physical activity not only makes the experience more fulfilling but also adds a layer of accountability and encouragement. Having friends to share the journey can turn exercise from a solitary struggle into a communal joy.

Creating a Routine that Works for You

Time management and personal preferences play crucial roles in making physical activity a consistent part of your life.

Scheduling Time for Exercise

Just like you wouldn't miss a doctor's appointment, treating exercise with the same priority can make it a non-negotiable part of your routine. Dedicate specific times during the week for exercise, and honor those commitments.

Integrating Exercise into Daily Life

But exercise doesn't always have to be a separate task. Integrating physical activity into daily life can make it feel more natural. A dance session with your kids or a brisk walk during lunch breaks can turn mundane routines into opportunities for movement and enjoyment.

Understanding Your Body's Needs

Our bodies are unique, and what works for one person may not work for another. How can you tailor an exercise routine that meets your specific needs?

Consulting with Healthcare Professionals

Talking to your healthcare provider about your exercise plan is vital, especially when managing diabetes. Your health conditions, medications, and needs should guide your exercise decisions. Personalized guidance ensures that your physical activities align with your overall health goals.

Listening to Your Body

Lastly, listening to your body is crucial. If something feels off or uncomfortable, don't ignore it. Consult a professional if needed, and remember that physical activity should enhance your well-being, not hinder it.

As you explore the world of exercise, keep in mind that it's not a race. It's about finding a balance that aligns with your life, interests, and health goals. Whether through mindful walks, energetic dance classes, or soothing stretches, physical activity can be a celebration of life and a pathway to holistic well-being.

Physical activity and diabetes management are companions on your journey towards a fuller, healthier, and more vibrant life. It's not just what's on your plate but how you move and feel. So take a step, stretch, or dance, knowing that you're embracing a life infused with joy, awareness, and purpose.

Stress Management and Mindful Eating: Techniques for a Balanced Lifestyle

Stress management is vital because stress affects almost every system in the body, including the digestive, cardiovascular, and nervous systems. When stress levels rise, the body responds by releasing hormones like cortisol, which can increase blood sugar levels. For those with type 2 diabetes, this rise can be problematic and challenging to manage. Additionally, stress often leads to unhealthy eating habits, further compounding the issue.

But what is stress management? Simply put, it's the practice of recognizing and responding to stress in healthy ways. Recognizing stress begins with understanding the signs that you're feeling overwhelmed, anxious, or tense. These signs can be physical, like headaches or stomach problems, emotional, such as feelings of anger or sadness, or behavioral, such as overeating or withdrawing from friends and family. Responding to stress in healthy ways means finding techniques that work for you to reduce stress and increase relaxation. These techniques can be as simple as taking deep breaths, going for a walk, or spending time with loved ones. They can also be more structured, like practicing yoga, meditation, or other mindfulness practices.

Mindful eating is closely connected to stress management and is equally essential for those with type 2 diabetes. Mindful eating is the practice of being fully present and engaged during eating, paying attention to the flavors, textures, and smells of your food, and listening to your body's hunger and fullness cues.

This practice can transform your relationship with food. Often, we eat in a rush or while distracted by other things, like watching TV or working on our computers. This mindless eating can lead to overeating and a disconnection from the physical experience of eating. It can also make it harder to make healthy food choices, as we're not paying attention to what and why we're eating.

Mindful eating slows down this process and brings awareness and intention to the act of eating. It allows you to recognize why you're eating – are you hungry, or are you eating out of stress, boredom, or some other emotion? By recognizing the why, you can make more intentional and healthy food choices.

But how do you practice mindful eating? Start by removing distractions during meals. Sit down at a table, away from your work or TV, and focus solely on your meal. Take time to look at your food, smell it, and taste it fully. Chew slowly, savoring each bite. Check in with yourself throughout your meal to see how full you're getting, and stop eating when you're satisfied, not when you're stuffed.

Mindful eating and stress management are both practices, meaning they take regular and continued effort. They are not something you do once and then forget about. Instead, they are ways of living and relating to yourself, your food, and your emotions. They require time, effort, and intention.

The benefits of these practices for those with type 2 diabetes are profound. By managing stress, you can keep your blood sugar levels more stable and enjoy a higher quality of life. By eating mindfully, you can make healthier food choices and have a more joyful and connected eating experience.

But more than that, these practices can transform your relationship with yourself. By recognizing and responding to stress in healthy ways, you're taking care of yourself. By eating mindfully, you're honoring and respecting your body. These acts of self-care can lead to increased self-esteem, confidence, and overall well-being, all of which can support your journey with type 2 diabetes.

In conclusion, stress management and mindful eating are essential techniques for those with type 2 diabetes. They are not standalone strategies but are interconnected and part of a broader approach to a balanced lifestyle. By integrating these practices into your daily life, you're not only better equipped to manage your diabetes, but you're also taking steps towards a more joyful, intentional, and connected life. These practices represent a shift away from simply treating symptoms and towards a more holistic, mindful approach to living. They are not quick fixes but ongoing practices that can lead to profound and lasting changes.

Regular Health Check-ups and Monitoring Blood Sugar Levels: What to Expect

Managing type 2 diabetes is a journey, one that requires diligent care, awareness, and proactive involvement. Two vital components of this journey are regular health check-ups and monitoring blood sugar levels. These practices are not merely occasional necessities; they're integral parts of daily living for someone striving to control and live healthily with diabetes.

Understanding the Importance of Regular Health Check-ups
Regular health check-ups are more than just a routine procedure. They are opportunities for healthcare providers to assess how well diabetes is being managed and to detect any potential complications early. These check-ups often go beyond blood sugar levels, including evaluating blood pressure, cholesterol levels, eye examinations, foot care, and more.

The eye, kidney, heart, and feet are particularly vulnerable to complications from diabetes. Regular screenings for these parts of the body can catch early signs of trouble, often before you even notice any symptoms, and allow for early intervention. Early intervention can prevent or slow down the progression of these complications, leading to better outcomes and quality of life.

Blood Sugar Monitoring: A Daily Routine

Monitoring blood sugar levels at home is another vital aspect of diabetes management. Knowing your blood sugar levels enables you to make informed decisions about your food, exercise, and medication. It's like having a continuous dialogue with your body, understanding its reactions and needs, and adjusting your daily routines accordingly.

A glucose meter is typically used for home monitoring. It requires a small blood sample, usually obtained by pricking your finger with a small, specially designed needle. The blood is then applied to a test strip that's inserted into the meter, and the glucose level is displayed.

But what should you expect from this practice? Initially, pricking your finger can be a little uncomfortable, but most people get used to it quickly. And the information you gain from these readings is invaluable.

For instance, if your blood sugar is higher than usual after a meal, you might decide to go for a walk or adjust your next meal to bring it down. If it's lower than expected, you might need to eat a small snack to prevent it from going too low.

So, what can you expect from regular health check-ups and blood sugar monitoring?

Your healthcare provider is your partner in managing diabetes. Regular check-ups are opportunities to discuss concerns, ask questions, and develop or adjust your treatment plan. Monitoring your blood sugar levels gives you immediate feedback on how different foods, activities, and medications affect your glucose levels. It allows you to take an active role in managing your condition. Though regular finger pricks and various screenings might seem daunting initially, the long-term benefits far outweigh the momentary discomfort.

Regular check-ups are not merely diagnostic; they are preventive. Catching potential complications early means they can often be treated more effectively. Regular interactions with healthcare professionals offer continuous education and support, helping you make informed decisions about your care.

Chapter 7: Resources

Glossary of Terms: Definitions of Key Terms

Introduction

Type 2 Diabetes: A chronic condition where the body either resists the effects of insulin or doesn't produce enough insulin to maintain normal glucose levels.
Insulin: A hormone produced by the pancreas that regulates the amount of glucose in the blood.
Glucose: A type of sugar found in the blood, used by the body's cells for energy.
Blood Sugar Level: The concentration of glucose present in the blood at any given time.
Hyperglycemia: High blood sugar levels, which can be dangerous if persistently high.
Hypoglycemia: Low blood sugar levels, which can also be harmful.
Insulin Resistance: A condition where the body's cells don't respond properly to insulin, leading to elevated blood sugar levels.

Dietary Terms
Carbohydrates: One of the primary types of nutrients that the body breaks down into glucose for energy.
Glycemic Index (GI): A measure of how quickly a food containing carbohydrates raises blood sugar levels.
Proteins: Essential nutrients found in animal products and some plant foods that support cell growth and repair.
Fats: Nutrients that provide energy, support cell growth, and help with the absorption of some vitamins.
Fiber: A type of carbohydrate that the body cannot digest, which helps with digestion and can regulate blood sugar levels.
Portion Control: The practice of controlling the size and content of meals to align with nutritional needs and goals.
Nutrient-Dense Foods: Foods that provide high levels of vitamins, minerals, and other beneficial substances relative to their calorie content.

Cookbook and Cooking Terms
Diabetes-Friendly Eating: A dietary approach that emphasizes foods and cooking methods suitable for managing blood sugar levels.
Meal Planning: The practice of planning meals ahead of time to ensure nutritional balance and align with specific dietary goals.
Substitution: Replacing an ingredient with another to align with dietary needs or

preferences, such as using a sugar substitute.

Cooking Techniques (e.g., Sautéing, Steaming): Specific methods used in cooking to prepare food, each affecting the flavor, texture, and nutritional content differently.

Emotional and Lifestyle Terms

Mindful Eating: A practice of being fully present and engaged during eating, recognizing feelings, sensations, and tastes.

Wellness: A holistic approach to health that considers physical, emotional, mental, and spiritual well-being.

Lifestyle Management: Integrating habits, practices, and routines that support overall health and well-being, including diet, exercise, stress management, and more.

Chapter 2: Getting Started

Kitchen Setup and Tools

Utensils: Implements, containers, or tools used in cooking, such as spatulas, ladles, and knives.

Pantry Staples: Basic ingredients that are commonly kept on hand in the kitchen pantry, such as flour, sugar substitutes, whole grains, and healthy oils.

Organization: The process of arranging kitchen tools and ingredients in a systematic and accessible manner to streamline cooking.

Cooking Techniques

Steaming: Cooking method that uses hot steam to gently cook food, preserving its texture and nutritional value.

Sautéing: Quick cooking method using a small amount of oil or fat in a pan over high heat, often used for vegetables or small pieces of meat.

Simmering: Cooking food gently in liquid just below the boiling point.

Roasting: Cooking method that uses dry heat, usually in an oven, to cook food evenly.

Grilling: Cooking food on a grill over an open flame or heat source.

Baking: Cooking food by surrounding it with dry heat in an oven.

Blanching: Briefly boiling food, then immediately cooling it in an ice bath to retain color and texture.

Nutritional Information

Carbohydrates: Organic compounds that are an essential energy source, including sugars, fibers, and starches.

Protein: Essential nutrients made of amino acids that support growth, maintenance, and repair in the body.

Fats: Nutrients that provide energy, support cell growth, and aid in nutrient absorption.

Food Labels: Information found on food packaging that provides details about the product's nutritional content, ingredients, and more.

Glycemic Index: A ranking of carbohydrates in foods according to how they affect blood sugar levels.

Mindful Cooking

Mindfulness: The practice of being present and fully engaging with the current moment, applied to cooking to enhance enjoyment and awareness.

Creativity: The use of imagination and originality in cooking, leading to unique and personalized dishes.

Wellness: A holistic approach to health that includes physical, mental, and emotional well-being, and can be supported through mindful cooking and eating.

Chapter 3: The 30-Day Meal Plan

Diabetes-Friendly Eating

Diabetes-Friendly Diet: A way of eating that includes foods and drinks that are beneficial for managing blood sugar levels, generally high in fiber and low in unhealthy fats and simple sugars.

Glycemic Index (GI): A ranking of carbohydrates on a scale from 0 to 100 according to how quickly they raise blood sugar levels when eaten. Lower GI foods are preferable for those with diabetes.

Portion Control: The practice of understanding and managing the amounts of food consumed in one sitting. This helps in maintaining a balanced diet and controlling blood sugar levels.

Variety and Balance

Macronutrients: The three main components of a diet, including carbohydrates, proteins, and fats. A balanced proportion of these is essential for a nutritious diet.

Micronutrients: Essential vitamins and minerals required in smaller quantities that support overall health.

Diverse Diet: Including a wide range of foods from different food groups to ensure nutritional completeness and satisfaction.

Portion Control

Serving Size: A standardized amount of food that allows for comparisons of nutrients in similar and dissimilar foods.

Portion Distortion: A situation where portion sizes are consistently larger than recommended, leading to overeating.

Food Scale: A tool that can be used to accurately measure the weight of food items to understand serving sizes better.

Building Confidence and Sustainability

Sustainable Eating Habits: A way of eating that can be maintained over the long term without undue hardship or sense of deprivation.

Supportive Environment: Creating or seeking a network of friends, family, or community members that encourage and help maintain healthy eating habits.

Health and Well-being Focus: An approach that emphasizes overall health, including physical activity, sleep, and stress management, in addition to diet.

General Terms

Blood Sugar Level: The amount of glucose present in the blood. Controlling this level is crucial for managing diabetes.

Insulin Resistance: A condition where the body's cells don't respond properly to insulin, leading to elevated blood sugar levels. This is common in type 2 diabetes.

Type 2 Diabetes: A chronic condition affecting the way the body processes glucose (sugar). It's characterized by insulin resistance or a lack of insulin production.

Chapter 6: Beyond the Kitchen

Physical Activity and Diabetes Management

Physical Activity: Any bodily movement that requires energy expenditure. This includes not only planned exercise but also daily activities like walking, gardening, or dancing.

Blood Sugar Control: The act of maintaining blood glucose levels within a normal range through a combination of diet, exercise, and medication.

Aerobic Exercise: Exercises that increase heart rate and breathing, such as walking, jogging, swimming, or biking, often beneficial for cardiovascular health.

Strength Training: Exercises focused on building muscle, such as weight lifting or bodyweight exercises. These can help with metabolism and blood sugar management.

Stress Management and Mindful Eating

Stress Management: Techniques and strategies used to cope with or lessen physical or emotional stress. This may include practices like meditation, deep breathing, or engaging in hobbies.

Mindful Eating: The practice of paying full attention to the eating experience, acknowledging the taste, texture, and aroma of the food, and being fully present during meals.

Emotional Eating: The act of eating in response to emotional needs rather than physical hunger, often tied to stress or other emotions.

Regular Health Check-ups and Monitoring Blood Sugar Levels

Health Check-up: Regular visits to healthcare providers for examinations, tests, and consultations, aiming to prevent or catch early any potential health issues.

Blood Sugar Monitoring: The process of checking blood glucose levels at different times, using a blood glucose meter. It helps in understanding how different factors like food, exercise, and medication affect blood sugar levels.

Glycated Hemoglobin (A1C) Test: A blood test that provides information about a person's average levels of blood glucose over the past 3 months. It's a crucial test for managing diabetes.

Fasting Blood Sugar (FBS) Test: A blood test that measures blood sugar levels after an overnight fast. It is often used to diagnose and monitor diabetes.

Hypoglycemia: A condition characterized by abnormally low blood sugar levels, which can lead to symptoms like dizziness, confusion, and in extreme cases, unconsciousness.

Hyperglycemia: A condition characterized by abnormally high blood sugar levels, which can lead to complications if persistently high.

Insulin: A hormone produced by the pancreas that regulates the amount of glucose in the blood. People with type 2 diabetes may have resistance to insulin or a deficiency in its production.

Recommended Food Brands for Diabetes: Trusted Options

The quest for nutritious, satisfying, and diabetes-friendly food can sometimes feel like a challenge. Yet, it's a journey that is both rewarding and essential for maintaining optimal health for those living with type 2 diabetes. Among the plethora of food brands available on supermarket shelves, discerning the options that align with diabetes-friendly eating requires careful consideration. In this section, we will delve into the world of trusted options and provide insights into recommended food brands for diabetes, without getting lost in the labyrinth of labels and nutritional charts.

Understanding what constitutes a diabetes-friendly food is paramount. People with diabetes must pay close attention to carbohydrates, fats, sugars, and overall nutrient content. Ensuring a balance of these elements helps in managing blood sugar levels. As we move forward, let's remember this balance and explore some of the key attributes that make certain food brands more suitable for those with diabetes.

Transparency and Integrity: Recommended brands for diabetes clearly state nutritional content, including carbohydrates, fats, and sugar. They provide detailed ingredient lists and prioritize whole, natural ingredients.

Low Glycemic Index: These brands offer products that release glucose slowly, aiding in blood sugar control.

Healthy Fats: Brands that use sources like olive oil, avocados, nuts, and seeds are aligned with diabetes nutrition.

Whole Grains and Fiber: Consider brands offering whole grain options and high-fiber products, as these help in controlling blood sugar levels.
Sodium and Additives: Brands that limit salt and unnecessary additives are preferable for a diabetes-friendly diet.

Personalization and Exploration: Individual needs vary, so engaging with trusted nutritionists or healthcare providers for personal recommendations encourages the exploration of new brands and products that suit personal taste and nutritional needs.

Additional Reading and Support Groups: Further Help

This section aims to guide you through additional reading and support groups, providing further assistance on this journey. Here, we're not only talking about recipes or exercise routines but also building bridges to communities and literature that can enrich understanding and foster a sense of belonging.

Expanding Knowledge Through Reading

Sometimes, the path to a healthier life begins with the turn of a page. Books, magazines, and online articles written by experts in the field of diabetes care can be a goldmine of information. Understanding diabetes is empowering, and it enables individuals to make informed decisions about their health.

Books

Numerous books cater specifically to those with diabetes, offering insights into managing the condition, understanding its biological underpinnings, and providing delicious, diabetes-friendly recipes. These books may range from scientifically in-depth literature to more accessible guides that speak directly to everyday concerns and challenges.

Magazines and Journals

Subscribing to magazines or journals that focus on health, nutrition, and diabetes can also be a rewarding way to stay up to date with the latest trends, research, and advice. The continual influx of information helps in aligning current practices with emerging knowledge.

Online Resources

In this digital age, reputable websites and blogs offer immediate access to a vast array of information. Here, personal stories often interweave with professional advice, creating a rich tapestry of insights and experiences.

Connection and Compassion Through Support Groups

While reading can provide knowledge, support groups offer a sense of community and emotional sustenance. Living with diabetes can sometimes feel isolating, but being part of a support group reminds you that you're not alone.

Local Support Groups

Local support groups often meet in community centers or healthcare facilities. These gatherings are more than just information sessions; they are a place to share, to listen, and to connect. The collective wisdom of those who have been navigating the path of diabetes can be both enlightening and comforting.

Online Communities

For those who may find attending physical meetings challenging, online communities offer an alternative space for connection and support. These virtual groups allow members to engage with others across the globe, broadening perspectives and fostering a sense of global solidarity.

Professional Guidance

Support groups often include healthcare professionals who can provide medical insights and advice tailored to individual needs. This professional guidance adds another layer of trust and understanding to the group experience.

Finding the Right Balance

In seeking additional reading and engaging with support groups, it's crucial to find what resonates with you personally. Each person's journey with diabetes is unique, and what works for one may not be suitable for another. It's a process of exploration, curiosity, and personal connection.

Chapter 7, "Resources," has taken us beyond the usual confines of medical management and dietary control. It has introduced us to a world filled with the warmth of community, the wisdom of literature, and the practicality of knowing the right brands to trust. The journey with type 2 diabetes, as we have explored, is as complex as it is personal, and this chapter has aimed to provide you with tools that resonate with both your physical needs and emotional well-being.

From understanding the brands that align with your health goals to connecting with people who share your journey, this chapter is a testament to the fact that managing diabetes is not a solitary endeavor. It's about building bridges with others, seeking knowledge, and finding comfort and strength in community and literature.

The tools and insights provided here are not just informational but transformational. They equip you not only to cope but to thrive, to see beyond the restrictions and to find joy, companionship, and empowerment. The resources highlighted offer a way to personalize your path, to make it not just about disease management but about living fully, richly, and with a sense of agency and connection.

In the grand mosaic of managing type 2 diabetes, this chapter adds color, texture, and depth. It recognizes the humanity behind the disease, the desire to know more, to connect, and to find support. It's about going beyond mere survival and stepping into a life that's enriched, engaged, and informed.

As you continue your journey with diabetes, let these resources be your guideposts, your companions, and your inspiration. Embrace the practical, the personal, and the profound, and know that you are more than the sum of dietary guidelines or medical prescriptions.

Appendices

Nutritional Information for Common Foods: A Handy Reference

An apple a day keeps the doctor away, so the adage goes, but what makes an apple, or any other food, beneficial or harmful? The answers lie in the complex web of nutritional values that define each food item. From the energy-providing carbohydrates to the essential vitamins and minerals, each element plays a crucial role in shaping our health.

The nutrients in foods are like the diverse threads of a tapestry, each contributing a unique color and texture. Carbohydrates, for instance, are often demonized in popular culture, but they are, in fact, a vital energy source. Proteins build and repair tissues, while fats, though controversial, are essential for absorbing certain vitamins. Vitamins and minerals, those minute but mighty nutrients, contribute to various bodily functions, from strengthening bones to boosting immunity.

The Dynamics of Nutritional Choices for Type 2 Diabetes

When it comes to diabetes management, the story becomes more nuanced. It's not just about counting calories or avoiding fats; it's about understanding the quality of carbohydrates, the type of fats, and the balance of proteins, vitamins, and minerals. Carbohydrates, especially complex ones found in whole grains, are a vital part of the diet, providing steady energy without spiking blood sugar levels. The fats, though necessary, must be chosen wisely, focusing on heart-healthy unsaturated fats found in foods like avocados and nuts. Proteins, while essential, must be balanced with fiber and vitamins to ensure a well-rounded diet.

Understanding the Glycemic Index (GI), a tool that ranks foods based on how quickly they raise blood sugar levels, adds another layer to this picture. Foods with a low GI, such as whole grains and certain fruits and vegetables, are often more suitable for people with type 2 diabetes.

Making Nutritional Information Accessible

Providing a detailed nutritional analysis of every food item would be overwhelming, but crafting a tapestry of understanding requires painting broad strokes. Let's delve into some examples that can act as guiding lights in your culinary journey.

Whole grains, such as brown rice or quinoa, are rich in complex carbohydrates, fiber, and various vitamins and minerals. They provide steady energy without causing rapid spikes in blood sugar, making them an integral part of a diabetes-friendly diet.

Vegetables, particularly non-starchy ones like leafy greens, peppers, and broccoli, are packed with vitamins, minerals, and fiber. They offer a nutritional punch without significantly affecting blood sugar levels.

Fruits, while rich in natural sugars, also offer vitamins, minerals, and fiber. Choosing whole fruits over juices and being mindful of portions can make them a healthy part of your diet.

Lean proteins such as chicken, fish, and tofu provide essential amino acids without the saturated fats found in fatty meats. Coupled with healthy fats like olive oil and avocados, they can form the cornerstone of a nutritious meal.

Substitution Chart for Common Ingredients: Alternatives for Dietary Restrictions

Sugars and Sweeteners:
- Sugar → Stevia, Monk Fruit Extract, Unsweetened Applesauce
- Honey → Agave Nectar (in smaller quantities), Sugar-Free Maple Syrup

Flours and Grains:
- White Flour → Whole Wheat Flour, Almond Flour, Oat Flour
- Regular Pasta → Whole Wheat Pasta, Spaghetti Squash, Zucchini Noodles

Dairy Alternatives:
- Milk → Almond Milk, Coconut Milk, Soy Milk
- Sour Cream → Greek Yogurt, Avocado

Fats and Oils:
- Butter → Olive Oil, Avocado Oil, Coconut Oil
- Margarine → Plant-Based Spreads, Nut Butters

Meats and Proteins:
- Red Meat → Lean Poultry, Fish, Tofu
- Full-Fat Cheese → Low-Fat or Skim Cheese, Nutritional Yeast

Salt and Seasonings:
- Salt → Herbs, Spices, Lemon Juice, Vinegar
- Soy Sauce → Low-Sodium Soy Sauce, Tamari

Cooking Fats:
- Shortening → Coconut Oil, Greek Yogurt
- Mayonnaise → Avocado, Hummus

Alcohol and Beverages:
- Regular Soda → Sparkling Water with a Splash of Lemon or Lime
- Alcohol → Non-Alcoholic Alternatives, Herbal Teas

Miscellaneous Substitutes:
- Chocolate Chips → Dark Chocolate Chips or Cacao Nibs
- Eggs in Baking → Mashed Banana, Unsweetened Applesauce

Shopping List Templates: For Easy Grocery Shopping

Date: [Insert Date] **Store:** [Insert Preferred Store]
Meal Plan for the Week:
- **Monday:** [Insert Meals]
- **Tuesday:** [Insert Meals]
- **Wednesday:** [Insert Meals]
- **Thursday:** [Insert Meals]
- **Friday:** [Insert Meals]
- **Saturday:** [Insert Meals]
- **Sunday:** [Insert Meals]

Fruits & Vegetables:
- Item 1: [Insert Name, Quantity]
- Item 2: [Insert Name, Quantity]
- ...

Grains & Cereals:
- Item 1: [Insert Name, Quantity]
- Item 2: [Insert Name, Quantity]
- ...

Proteins:
- Item 1: [Insert Name, Quantity]
- Item 2: [Insert Name, Quantity]
- ...

Dairy & Alternatives:
- Item 1: [Insert Name, Quantity]
- Item 2: [Insert Name, Quantity]
- ...

Healthy Fats:
- Item 1: [Insert Name, Quantity]
- Item 2: [Insert Name, Quantity]
- ...

Snacks & Others:
- Item 1: [Insert Name, Quantity]
- Item 2: [Insert Name, Quantity]
- ...

Special Notes:
- [Insert any special instructions, reminders, or substitutions]

Measurement And Conversion Table

Volume

Measurement	Equals	Also Equals
1 cup	8 fluid ounces	237 milliliters
1 pint (2 cups)	16 fluid ounces	473 milliliters
1 quart (2 pints)	32 fluid ounces	946 milliliters
1 gallon (4 quarts)	128 fluid ounces	3.785 liters

Weight

Measurement	Equals	Also Equals
1 ounce	1/16 pound	28.35 grams
1 pound	16 ounces	453.59 grams

Cooking Measures

Measurement	Equals	Also Equals
1 tablespoon	3 teaspoons	15 milliliters
1 cup	16 tablespoons	237 milliliters
1 fluid ounce	2 tablespoons	29.57 milliliters

Oven Temperatures:

Measurement Fahrenheit	Equals Celsius
225°F	110°C
250°F	130°C
275°F	140°C
300°F	150°C
325°F	165°C
350°F	180°C
375°F	190°C
400°F	200°C
425°F	220°C
450°F	230°C
475°F	245°C
500°F	260°C

Dry Measures:

Measurement	Equals	Also Equals
1 ounce	28.35 grams	
1 pound	16 ounces	453.59 grams

Index

Alphabetical Listing of Recipes and Key Topics

Cinnamon Roasted Nuts
Classic Chicken Noodle Soup
Creamy Mushroom Soup
Cucumber and Hummus Sandwich

E

Egg Salad Sandwich
Eggplant and Tomato Stew

F

Farro with Lemon and Spinach
Fresh Berry Salad

G

Garlic Roasted Asparagus
Garlic Shrimp Zoodle Bowl
Grilled Asparagus and Lemon Salad
Grilled Chicken Caesar Salad
Grilled Lemon Herb Chicken Breast
Grilled Pineapple with Coconut
Grilled Pork Chops with Apple Sauce
Grilled Pork Chops with Green Beans
Grilled Shrimp and Pineapple Skewers
Grilled Vegetable Panini
Grilled Vegetable Skewers
Green Delight Smoothie
Greek Yogurt with Fresh Berries

L

Lentil and Tomato Soup
Lentil Soup
Lentil Spinach Soup
Lemon Chia Seed Cake
Lemon Garlic Tilapia
Lemon Zucchini Noodles

M

Mediterranean Chickpea Salad
Millet Stir-Fry with Mixed Veggies
Mocha Morning Drink
Multigrain Pancakes with Berries

O

Overnight Oats with Almond Milk

P

Peach Yogurt Parfait
Pear and Arugula Salad with Feta
Pork Chops with Sautéed Spinach
Pumpkin Spice Cookies

Q

Quinoa and Roasted Veggie Bowl
Quinoa and Roasted Vegetable Salad

Quinoa Breakfast Bowl
Quinoa Salad with Tomatoes and Basil

R

Raspberry Almond Smoothie
Roast Beef and Veggie Rolls

S

Shrimp and Avocado Salad
Shrimp and Vegetable Stir-Fry
Slow-Cooker Pulled Pork Lettuce Wraps
Smoked Salmon and Cream Cheese Wrap
Spaghetti Squash with Pesto
Spinach and Mushroom Quiche
Spinach and Potato Soup
Spinach Stuffed Chicken Breast
Stuffed Acorn Squash
Stuffed Bell Peppers
Sugar-Free Chocolate Brownie
Steak and Green Bean Sauté

T

Thai Beef Salad
Tuna and Cucumber Boats
Tuna Salad Sandwich
Turkey Avocado Wrap
Turkey Lettuce Wraps

V

Vegan Lentil and Mushroom Burger
Vegan Tofu Scramble
Veggie Omelette
Veggie Sticks with Hummus Dip

W

Whole Grain Penne with Roasted Vegetables
Whole Wheat Breakfast Burrito

Z

Zucchini Noodles with Tomato Sauce